FACTS AT YOUR FINGERTIPS

ANCIENT
GREECE

BROWN
BEAR
BOOKS

Published by Brown Bear Books Limited

An imprint of:
The Brown Reference Group Ltd
68 Topstone Road
Redding
Connecticut 06896
USA

www.brownreference.com

© 2009 The Brown Reference Group Ltd

Library of Congress Cataloging-in-Publication Data
available upon request

ISBN-13 978-1-933834-55-9

Editorial Director: Lindsey Lowe
Managing Editor: Tim Cooke
Design Manager: David Poole
Designer: Sarah Williams
Picture Manager: Sophie Mortimer
Picture Researcher: Sean Hannaway
Text Editor: Anita Dalal
Indexer: Indexing Specialists (UK) Ltd

Printed in the United States of America

CONTENTS

INTRODUCTION

This book is about the ancient Greeks. They were perhaps the most restless, adventurous, and creative people who have ever lived. In ancient times Greek towns and villages stretched far beyond the small country we now know as Greece. In the late fourth century BCE Alexander the Great, with his Greek-speaking troops, conquered a territory from Asia Minor and Egypt in the west to India in the east.

Our book has many maps to help you keep track of what Greeks in different places were doing. To understand the Greeks, maps are even more important than they are for most other civilizations. Greece, for most of its long history, had no capital city and no single government. Instead, there were dozens, sometimes even hundreds, of independent Greek communities. These are called "city-states." But probably only two of them, Athens and Alexandria, grew as big as a modern city.

Independent communities

If we could travel back through time and visit a typical Greek community, it would seem to us more like a village than a city. Yet a large village in ancient Greece often had its own defensive wall, and made its own decisions on big issues, such as whether to go to war. The independence of these communities probably helped their citizens feel that their views mattered. This self-confidence encouraged many Greeks to be creative.

Abbreviations used in this book

BCE = Before Common Era (also known as BC)
CE = Common Era (also known as AD)
c. = circa (about)
in = inch; ft = foot; mi = mile
cm = centimeter; m = meter; km = kilometer

When referring to dates, early third century BCE, for example, means about 290 or 280 BCE, and late third century BCE means about 220 or 210 BCE.

The spelling of Greek names adopted in this book uses the *k* form (with *-os* and *-on* endings) rather than the alternative *c* form (with *-us* and *-um* endings).

Lasting ideas

The ideas of the Greeks spread very widely. From the second century BCE most Greek communities were eventually taken into the empire of Rome. But so clever and educated were many Greeks that they found themselves educating their Roman masters. They taught the Romans how to write, paint, build, and even how to run the Roman Empire. Today the Greeks are definitely in fashion. This is because there is great respect for new ideas, and Greece excelled in producing new ideas that would last. "Drama," "athletics," "philosophy," "democracy" are all words of Greek origin for things that were invented by the ancient Greeks.

Our book looks at the most famous periods of ancient Greek history, from 1600 BCE (the late Bronze Age) down to around 100 BCE, the time of the Roman conquest. In this long stretch of time, Greek civilization took strikingly different forms. For example, Mycenaean Greeks of the Bronze Age are famous for their beautiful paintings and metalwork, and for the script in which they wrote—Linear B. By the eighth century BCE, the Greeks had forgotten Linear B. Instead, they used a very different script, the first letters of which were alpha and beta, the basis of the alphabet that we use today.

Structure of the book

Ancient Greece is divided into two main sections. The first tells the story of the Greeks and describes how they gradually became an important world power. Throughout this section there are maps illustrating themes or topics in the main text, together with guides to specific archaeological sites. Many are accompanied by charts giving important dates and events in Greek history. The second part, Culture and Society, tells us more about how the Greeks lived, the gods and goddesses they worshiped, and the military strength that helped build their empire.

A few columns have been reconstructed of the Philippeion at Olympia, site of the original Olympic Games. The memorial was built to honor the military victories of the fourth-century BCE king Philip of Macedonia. It contained statues of Philip and his family, including his son Alexander the Great.

TIMELINES

	2000 BCE	1500 BCE	1000 BCE	800 BCE	600 BCE
CULTURAL PERIOD	Bronze age		Dark age	Archaic period	

AEGEAN AND GREEK MAINLAND

Cretan palace civilization

Shaft graves at Mycenae

Explosion at Santorini

Fall of Knossos

Fall of Mycenaeans

Iron introduced from East then return to bronze

Rise of aristocratic families

Population increases in Greece

Chief period of colonization to E and W

International festivals established

Tyrants in control of many cities

Invention of hoplite fighting

First Greek coins

Beginnings of democracy at Athe[ns]

Sparta dominate[s] Peloponn[ese]

So-called mask of Agamemnon from Mycenae, 1550–1500 BCE.

The "warrior vase" from Mycenae, early 12th century BCE.

Geometric amphora from Athens, c.750 BCE.

The "peplos kore" from the Athenian Akropolis, c.530 BCE.

POTTERY STYLE ART AND ARCHITECTURE

Great palaces in Crete

Figurines, fine working in gold and semiprecious stones (e.g. sealstones)

Santorini frescoes

Great beehive tombs

Sub-Mycenaean protogeometric

Geometric

Orientalizing

Monumental vases

Olympia tripods

First stone temples

Archaic (Athenian Black Figure)

Kouroi and korai

Octopus flask from eastern Crete, 1350 BCE.

13th-century BCE carved ivory from Mycenae.

Bronze statue of hoplite, Dodone.

LITERATURE, PHILOSOPHY, AND SCIENCE

Linear A tablets

Linear B tablets

Phoenician alphabet

Greek alphabet

Homer

Hesiod

Lyric poets

Beginnings of tragedy and comedy

Pythagoras

Sappho

EGYPT, ASIA MINOR, AND THE EAST

Egyptian New Kingdom

Great temples

Tutankhamon

Hittite Empire in Anatolia

Babylonian Empire

Greek colonies in Ionia, then around Black Sea

Assyrian Empire at most powerful

Assyrians lose power to Medes and Babylonians

Darius founds Persian Empire

Persians conqu[er] Egypt

Classical period	Hellenistic period		Roman Empire	Byzantine Empire

Persian invasions

Athens dominates
Delian League

Age of Perikles

Peloponnesian War

Athenian revival

Rise of Macedon

Fall of Sparta

Campaigns of
Alexander

Rise to power of
Achaean and
Aetolian leagues

Macedonian wars

Macedonia becomes Roman province

Achaea becomes Roman province

Greece remains cultural and intellectual
center of Mediterranean

*The Parthenon at Athens,
completed 441–432 BCE.*

*Alexander the Great at the battle
of Issos. Detail from the "Alexander
mosaic" found at Pompeii, copy of
a Greek painting c.300 BCE.*

*The Venus de
Milo, a second-
century BCE
marble statue
from Melos.*

*Roman coin of
Hadrian, second
century C.E.*

Athenian Red Figure

Temple of Zeus at Olympia

Parthenon, Erechtheion

Pheidias and Polykleitos (sculptors)

Polygnotos (painter)

South Italian painters

Praxiteles (sculptor)

Mausoleum at Halikarnassos

Hellenistic baroque

Altar of Zeus, Pergamon

Winged Victory of
Samothrace

Venus de Milo

Santa Sophia built
Constantinople (Istanbul)

Roman copying of Greek
sculpture and architecture

*Fifth-century BCE
vase with archaic
poets, Sappho
and Alkaios.*

*Silver coin
from Athens,
c.440 BCE.*

*Painted terracotta,
women gossiping,
c.320 BCE.*

*Bust of philosopher,
possibly Bion.*

Aischylos, Pindar, Sophokles,

Herodotos, Euripides,

Sokrates, Hippokrates,

Thucydides, Aristophanes

Plato, Aristotle,

Epicurus, Theokritos,

Euclid, Archimedes

Creation of library at Alexandria

Pausanias

Darius crosses Hellespont
and invades Greece

Alexander conquers Asia Minor,
Egypt, Persia, NW India

Successor kingdoms, Ptolemaic,
Seleukid dynasties

Gauls settle in Galatia (modern Turkey)

Parthian Empire founded

Rome defeats Antiochos of Syria

Pergamon becomes Roman province

Egypt becomes Roman province

Sasanian Empire founded in Persia

Byzantion refounded by
Romans (Constantinople)

MINOANS AND MYCENAEANS

The island of Crete in the Mediterranean Sea was home to the first major civilization of the Aegean, the Minoans. The Minoan civilization peaked between 2200 and 1450 BCE. From what we know, the Minoans were a peaceful people who grew rich from farming and trade. They traded with peoples from the Greek mainland and as far away as Egypt and Syria. The Minoans probably did not speak Greek.

At Knossos on Crete are the remains of the most famous structure from the Minoan period, the palace of Knossos. The palace was very big, with many beautiful rooms decorated with wall paintings. The paintings show scenes of life at court. One painting shows young people leaping in the air and performing somersaults between the horns of a bull.

The Mycenaeans

Around 1450 BCE, a new power emerged on Crete when the Mycenaeans, a Greek-speaking people, took control of the island. Writing on clay tablets, found at Knossos, has been proved to be Greek (archeologists call the script "Linear B"). Tablets found on the Greek mainland give some idea about life at this time. They record what was kept in the storehouses of the palaces and how wealth was distributed. The two greatest palaces on the mainland were at Mycenae and Pylos.

Between around 1600 and 1150 BCE, Greece was made up of small independent kingdoms, but today they are all known as "Mycenaean." The Mycenaeans copied much from the Minoans, particularly from its artists and craftsmen, but there was one big difference: The Mycenaeans were more warlike. Paintings show tall warrior kings driving in chariots to battle and hunting for lions and wild boar.

Modern houses cluster on the sides of the volcanic island of Santorini (Thera in Greek). Archaeologists have discovered evidence that the island was influenced by both the Minoans and the Mycenaeans. A huge eruption of Santorini destroyed the Minoan civilization in Crete in the mid-16th century BCE.

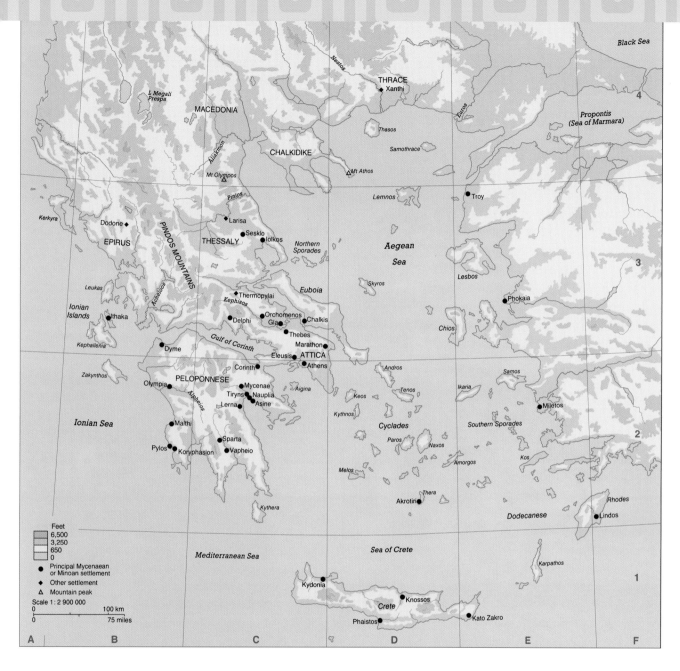

The map shows the Aegean Sea region in the Bronze Age, with labels including:

Black Sea, THRACE, Xanthi, MACEDONIA, L Megali Prespa, Nestos, Propontis (Sea of Marmara), Thasos, Samothrace, CHALKIDIKE, Mt Athos, Lemnos, Troy, Mt Olympos, Pinios, Larisa, Sesklo, Iolkos, Kerkyra, Dodone, EPIRUS, PINDOS MOUNTAINS, THESSALY, Northern Sporades, Aegean Sea, Lesbos, Leukas, Thermopylai, Kephisos, Euboia, Skyros, Ionian Islands, Ithaka, Delphi, Orchomenos, Gla, Chalkis, Phokaia, Kephallenia, Dyme, Gulf of Corinth, Thebes, Marathon, Chios, Acheloos, Eleusis, ATTICA, Corinth, Athens, Andros, Samos, Zakynthos, PELOPONNESE, Mycenae, Aigina, Tenos, Ikaria, Olympia, Tiryns, Nauplia, Keos, Miletos, Alpheios, Lerna, Asine, Kythnos, Cyclades, Southern Sporades, Malthi, Sparta, Paros, Naxos, Kos, Pylos, Koryphasion, Vapheio, Amorgos, Ionian Sea, Melos, Thera, Rhodes, Akrotiri, Dodecanese, Lindos, Karpathos, Kythera, Sea of Crete, Mediterranean Sea, Kydonia, Crete, Knossos, Kato Zakro, Phaistos

Feet
6,500
3,250
650
0
● Principal Mycenaean or Minoan settlement
♦ Other settlement
△ Mountain peak
Scale 1 : 2 900 000
0 — 100 km
0 — 75 miles

The Aegean Sea in the Bronze Age. Crete, in the south, was the home of the Minoan civilization, which the Greeks of the mainland both conquered and copied. Mycenae, on the southern part of the mainland, has left spectacular ruins from the late second millennium BCE (c.1300 BCE). However, many other Greek towns, such as Pylos, Sparta, and Gla, may have been independent of the gold-rich kings of Mycenae.

The Mycenaeans were skilled builders and artists. To protect the palaces, they used huge stones to make defensive walls. How the stones had been put in place puzzled the Greeks who followed centuries later. They concluded that a race of giants must have built the walls of the Mycenaean palaces.

Trade with Other Lands

The Mycenaeans were accomplished farmers and craftsmen but much of their riches came from trade. They traded with distant lands. Papyrus came from Egypt and amber, which was used in the making of jewelry, came from the Baltic Sea in northern Europe.

Knossos

The city of Knossos on the island of Crete is one of the western world's oldest cities. The city was at its height between 2000 and 1400 BCE. Its narrow streets were lined with small two-storied houses and up to 100,000 people may have lived there at its peak. The city's wealth came from trade. Goods were transported from its port, Amnisos (some 20 miles/32 km outside Knossos) to as far away as Egypt and Syria.

Today, Knossos is one of the world's foremost archeological sites. British archeologists led by Arthur Evans first excavated its palace in 1900 CE. Archeologists have uncovered evidence that the Minoans had developed a highly sophisticated civilization. The presence of clay pipes in the palace prove that it had running water.

The Palace at Knossos

The palace was made up of a lot of small rooms, which were built as and when they were needed. Some experts believe that the jumble of rooms in the palace basement lies behind the story of the Minotaur. This half-man, half-bull was said to live in a maze on Crete, where he fed off human sacrifices until he was defeated by the hero Theseus.

The island of Crete lies in an earthquake zone and a series of earthquakes have destroyed the palace. It is clear, however, that unlike the Mycenaean palaces, Knossos was not highly fortified, suggesting that the Minoans were not a warlike people.

Minoan influence

The Mycenaean Greeks later copied the Minoans' dress and art. Wall paintings found in Mycenaean palaces depict Cretan ladies dressed in low-cut dresses with puffed sleeves and flounced skirts. Historians think that because there are so many women in the paintings they must have held an important position within Minoan society. Some suggest that women's high status helped instill the importance of living peacefully.

Santorini

Santorini (Thera in Greek) is an island in the southern Aegean. It is volcanic in origin: the modern island forms a horseshoe

shape around what was once the rim of the volcano's crater. Archeologists have been working on the island since 1967 CE. They have uncovered the remains of houses that date from around 1500 BCE. It is clear that the houses belonged to wealthy people from the stunning paintings that decorate the walls. They were painted in the style of Minoan Crete and of Mycenae. The paintings are remarkably well preserved because they were covered in debris from a volcanic eruption when they were still quite fresh, thus preserving them.

The wall paintings tell stories that give us a good sense of the local civilization. In one painting, there are long, low warships with brightly colored canopies that are about to set off on a raid. Dolphins jump out of the water. The next image depicts the raiders arriving at a coastal town to attack its residents. Some of the towns' defenders are seen drowning. We see the targets of the raid: the raiders want to take women and animals from the town. Then the raiders are welcomed home by a group of men, while women watch from a flat roof. Some of the raiders are wearing boars' tusk helmets in the Mycenaean style.

Poetic echo

The pictorial story of a sea raid with important female characters echoes the later tales of the epic poet Homer. His Iliad and Odyssey tell of heroic Greek warriors crossing the sea to Asia Minor, in order to fight the Trojans and win back Helen of Troy.

Two boys boxing, in a painting from Santorini. Their tanned skin is shown in red.

Mycenae

The archeological remains of Ancient Greece tell us about how the richest people lived, but not about the poor, who made up the majority of the population. While the rich lived in houses made of stone, the poor lived in mud houses, which did not last. Similarly, the rich could afford beautiful jewelry crafted from precious metals and stones, while the poor had few possessions and what they owned was often made of perishable materials.

We know quite a lot about how the Mycenaean rulers lived because parts of their palaces and their contents have survived for more than 3,000 years. Historians have been able to build up a good picture of how the rich lived, but we know very little about the builders, artists, metalworkers, and stone carvers who worked on these palaces.

The riches of Mycenae

The town of Mycenae was located on the Greek mainland on a small hill in the northeastern Peloponnese, a few miles inland from the sea. The palace sat atop the hill allowing the rulers to keep an eye, not just on their villagers below, but also on potential attacks from their enemies.

The site of the town was well chosen, as there was a natural harbor close by. Goods that passed through on the way to Mycenae included copper and tin to make bronze weapons, gold and amber used for jewelry, papyrus for writing, and ivory for carving. The Mycenaeans were a warring people and they used the harbor to launch their warships, but it was harder for their enemies to attack them from the sea, because Mycenae was not on the coast.

The Lion Gate, the main entrance in the massive defensive wall of Mycenae. The picture shows the gate as 19th-century archeologists found it. Clearing away the earth and fallen stones has shown the gate to be much taller than it appears here.

Archeologists have discovered gold masks that were used to cover the faces of their dead rulers. Craftsmen started to create these masks from about 1600 BCE. onward. The level of craftsmanship was high and the masks give us a clear idea of what the rulers looked like in life. The craftsmen of Mycenae developed different styles, including carving curves on their ivory sculptures of women and giving a shape to stone lions. This style was first seen in Minoan sculptures from which the Mycenaeans copied. The stone roofs of the huge beehive-shaped tombs, in which the later Mycenaean rulers were placed, were also curved.

Pylos was an important Mycenaean town located in the southwestern Peloponnese. It was built close to one of the best natural harbors in Greece. Just as with Mycenae, we know a lot about the daily life of Pylos from inscriptions on clay tablets found at the site. These tablets record how goods were distributed and refer to the presence of guards on the coast. They were probably meant to protect against an attack from the sea.

One of the objects found at Pylos was a bathtub. The ruler of Pylos may have sat in it while his female slaves bathed him. Other treasures found at Pylos include carved ivory, which was set into wood.

The famous golden death mask from the royal graves at Mycenae. When the German archeologist Schliemann found it, in his excitement he thought that it showed the face of the legendary King Agamemnon. This now seems unlikely, however.

THE DARK AGE

Following the end of the Mycenaean period, Greece entered a period about which we know very little. For some reason, the building of palaces stopped and craftsmen no longer produced fine work. This Dark Age saw trade disrupted and people in the region grew poorer. Almost nothing flourished except the memories of the people. They remembered the glories of the Mycenaean Age and worked them into epic stories. Two of the most famous epics were most probably told countless times until the poet Homer wrote them down in the middle of the eighth century BCE. These epics are the *Iliad* and the *Odyssey*.

Between 1200 and 1150 BCE, an unknown enemy attacked the Mycenaean world. We know the Mycenaeans were attacked because of an account inscribed on a Linear B tablet from Pylos. It describes how men were positioned on the coast to look out for the enemy coming from the sea. Once the Mycenaean culture came under attack, its rulers ordered the building of its defensive walls. Rather than show the

Places of importance in the Dark Age of Ancient Greece. Emigrants were colonizing the western coast of Asia Minor. Some signs of life survived in the great centers of the Mycenaean past, such as Tiryns, Sparta, and Mycenae itself. Geometric pottery was made throughout Greece at this time.

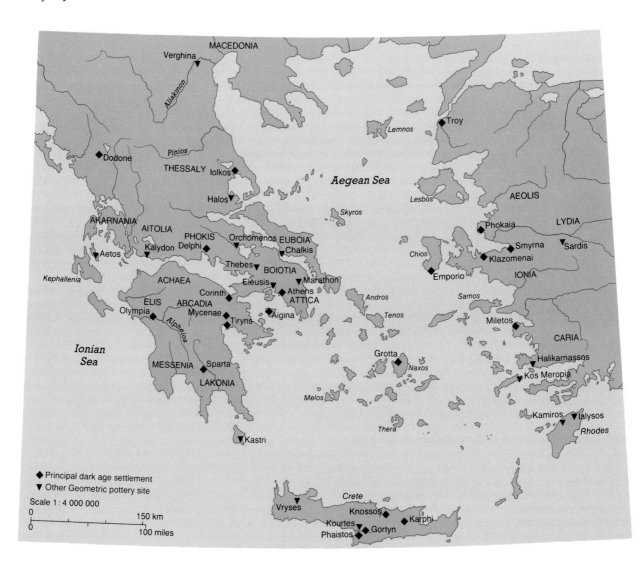

MACEDONIA
Verghina
Aliakmon
Troy
Lemnos
Pinios
Dodone
THESSALY Iolkos
Aegean Sea
Halos
Lesbos
AEOLIS
AKARNANIA
Skyros
AITOLIA
PHOKIS
Orchomenos EUBOIA
LYDIA
Kalydon Delphi
Chalkis
Phokaia
Aetos
Thebes
BOIOTIA
Chios
Smyrna
Sardis
Klazomenai
Kephallenia
ACHAEA
Eleusis
Marathon
Emporio
IONIA
Corinth
Athens
ELIS ARCADIA
ATTICA
Andros
Samos
Olympia
Mycenae
Aigina
Alpheios
Tiryns
Tenos
Miletos
Ionian
Sea
CARIA
Grotta
Halikarnassos
MESSENIA
Sparta
Naxos
Kos Meropia
LAKONIA
Melos
Kamiros
Ialysos
Thera
Rhodes
Kastri

◆ Principal dark age settlement
▼ Other Geometric pottery site

Scale 1 : 4 000 000
0   150 km
0   100 miles

Crete
Vryses
Knossos
Kourtes
Karphi
Phaistos
Gortyn

strength of the Mycenaeans, the walls showed their weakness and marked the beginning of the end of their power.

Remembering the Mycenaean Age

The poets of the Dark Age remembered the glories of the Mycenaean culture, the royal palaces at Mycenae and Pylos and the treasures of another city located in northwestern Asia Minor called Troy.

Much of the information about the Mycenaean culture found in the *Iliad* is broadly correct and has been backed up by archeological finds. For example, the *Iliad* recounts how armies from Mycenae and Pylos fought, with others, against Troy, laying siege to it for 10 years. The descriptions of the Mycenaean weapons and styles are probably fairly accurate. Another interesting detail is the description of single combat battles in which aristocratic leaders, such as Odysseus, Diomedes, Achilles, Aias (Ajax), and Menelaos, fought against enemy leaders. We learn they used "tower-tall" shields, threw spears, and traveled in chariots. This style of fighting contrasts with the later classical period, when soldiers marched into battle in long lines, carrying shields and spears for stabbing and not throwing. We know from archeological finds that the Mycenaeans did use chariots.

The map shows places and leaders that sent ships to make war on Troy.

Apart from fighting, the poets also knew how Mycenaean craftsmen used gold to make beautiful treasures, including the death masks. Life during the Dark Age may not have been as violent as the Mycenaean period. The *Iliad* tells us much about rural life, with many references to shepherds, woodcutters, and fishermen.

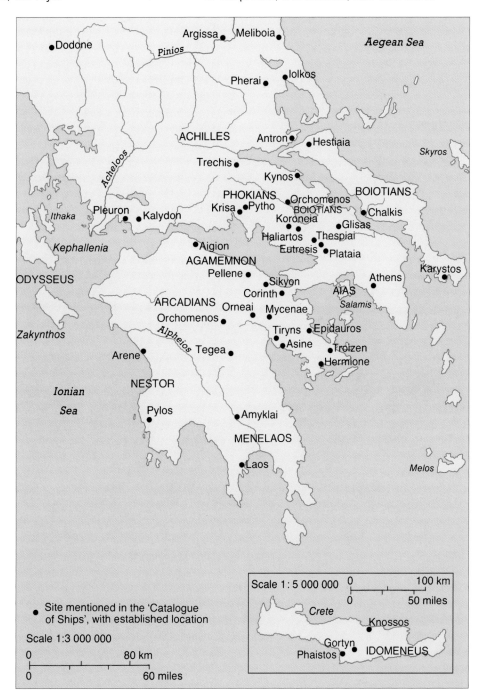

ARISTOCRATS AND POETS

When the Dark Age ended in about the eighth century BCE, the Aegean region flourished again. Greece was divided up into many small independent communities, mostly ruled by a group of very rich men. These men were the aristocrats. The Greeks referred to them as "the best" (*aristoi* in Greek), "the land sharers," or "the horse-breeders." These rich men owned the best land in their communities. When they died, their sons inherited the land.

Wealth and Horses

One symbol of an aristocrat's power and wealth was the horse. Horses were highly valued in Greek society. Sons of aristocrats were often given names with a horse reference. The Greek word for horse is *hippos*. Examples of Greek names include Xanthippos ("tawny horse") and Philippos ("horse-lover"). Horses were expensive, so only the rich could afford a good war horse. Horses were shown off in religious processions and, later, horse and chariot racing became popular sports. When an aristocrat died, his horse took part in his funeral procession.

Wine and Poetry

The rich men of early Greece liked to drink wine. To get drunk was a sign of wealth and was highly regarded. Only the rich could afford to buy wine. Drinking parties were known as a *symposion*. It was not unusual for a symposion to end up in an orgy (sex party) as pretty young slave women (*hetairai*) entertained the rich men.

Other parties were not so wild and men would recite poetry. A favorite party game of the early Greeks was making up poetry. The Greeks loved poetry and saw it as proof of their superior education. Professional poets also entertained the rich men at parties. They often made up poems that flattered their patrons. They did this by praising the ancestors of a rich man and suggesting they were connected to the gods.

Power of the Aristocrats

Early Greek society was shaped like a pyramid. At the top of the pyramid were a few very rich families who were served by the majority. They were made up of poor farmers, slaves, and craftsmen who did not like the inequality of their society. The poet Hesiod complained, in the early eighth century BCE, that when a rich

Places of importance in the age of the aristocrats. The poet Hesiod lived in the village of Askra and wrote that it was "hard in summer, bad in winter and never any good." The later poet Pindar, in contrast with Hesiod's bad feelings, wrote gushing praise of aristocrats and their lands.

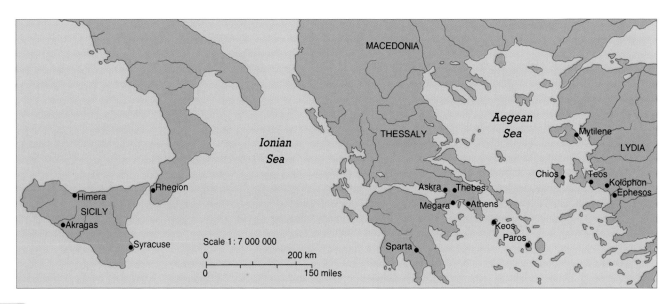

man had a quarrel with a poor man, the law was always on the side of the rich man.

The power of the aristocrats declined in the seventh century BCE. This was partly due to the rise of a new class of fighters, known as the hoplites, who created a new kind of warfare. The hoplites were heavily armed with spears and shields and fought in long lines on foot.

This formation was able to beat the aristocrats' cavalry, whose power started to fade.

A new power emerged between these two groups. Autocrats (*tyrannos*) began to grab power by taking aristocrats' lands. During the seventh and sixth centuries BCE, tyrants ruled city-states such as Corinth, Athens, and Miletos; no tyrant ever ruled Sparta.

A poet sings his verses to a party of aristocrats, accompanying himself on the lyre. The guests drink from hand-painted pottery. They are all men, and a favorite theme of the poetry they would hear was the manly pursuit of war and deeds of battle.

Many of the poets who helped compose the Iliad *and the* Odyssey *may have sung at parties like this. The two poems were certainly meant to please the rich. They usually show aristocratic characters as noble and heroic, while the character Thersites, who criticizes aristocrats, is described in the* Iliad *as ugly and ridiculous.*

COLONIZATION

Over time, Greek colonies could be found scattered across the Mediterranean and Black Sea coasts. Colonies were settled in the east in Asia Minor, in Italy, Sicily, and in the west in southern Spain. There were a few settlements in North Africa. The colonies never combined to create a great empire as the Romans would later make. Instead, Greek settlers usually established their communities close to the sea. The Greeks did not like to be too far inland.

Greek colonists did not want to conquer new lands; rather, they just wanted to survive. The father of the poet Hesiod left Greece around 750 BCE to find a new home "from wretched poverty". One problem back in Greece was the difficulty of growing food in the mountainous terrain. Many simply left to find better agricultural land. Inhabitants of the island of Thera sailed for Africa hoping to escape poverty and found a new colony. When their first attempt failed and returned to Thera, their former neighbors refused to let them ashore, stoning the ships to stop them landing.

It was difficult to found a new colony. The sea journey was hard, and if the Greeks made it to land there was always a chance the local people would attack them. In the 460s BCE, Athenians and other Greeks sent 10,000 men to found a new colony north of the Aegean. Non-Greeks attacked them and destroyed the colony.

The Spread of Greek Settlements

Colonization happened in fits and starts. After Mycenae fell, the Greeks turned to the east to settle in western Asia Minor and its islands. Between the eighth and sixth centuries BCE, the Greeks moved north and west. Colonies such as Miletos and Corinth founded new colonies. Miletos founded little colonies around the Black Sea, while Corinth founded Kerkyra (the island of Corfu) and Syracuse (in present-day Sicily) in the west. Sicily and southern Italy had so many Greek colonies that the region became known as "Magna Graecia" or "Great Greece."

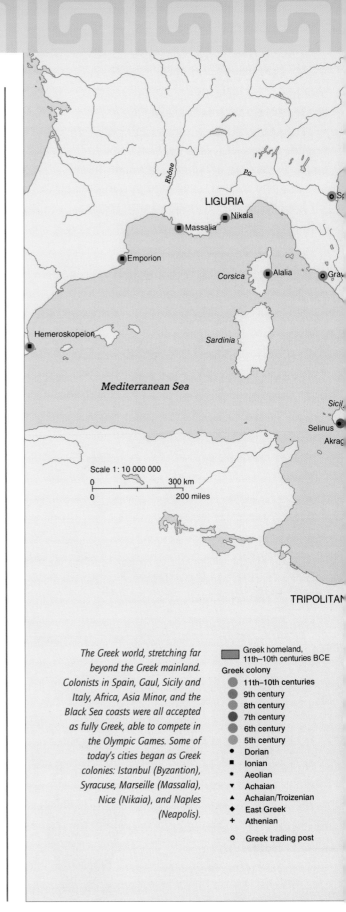

The Greek world, stretching far beyond the Greek mainland. Colonists in Spain, Gaul, Sicily and Italy, Africa, Asia Minor, and the Black Sea coasts were all accepted as fully Greek, able to compete in the Olympic Games. Some of today's cities began as Greek colonies: Istanbul (Byzantion), Syracuse, Marseille (Massalia), Nice (Nikaia), and Naples (Neapolis).

Greek homeland, 11th–10th centuries BCE

Greek colony
- 11th–10th centuries
- 9th century
- 8th century
- 7th century
- 6th century
- 5th century
- Dorian
- Ionian
- Aeolian
- Achaian
- Achaian/Troizenian
- East Greek
- Athenian
- Greek trading post

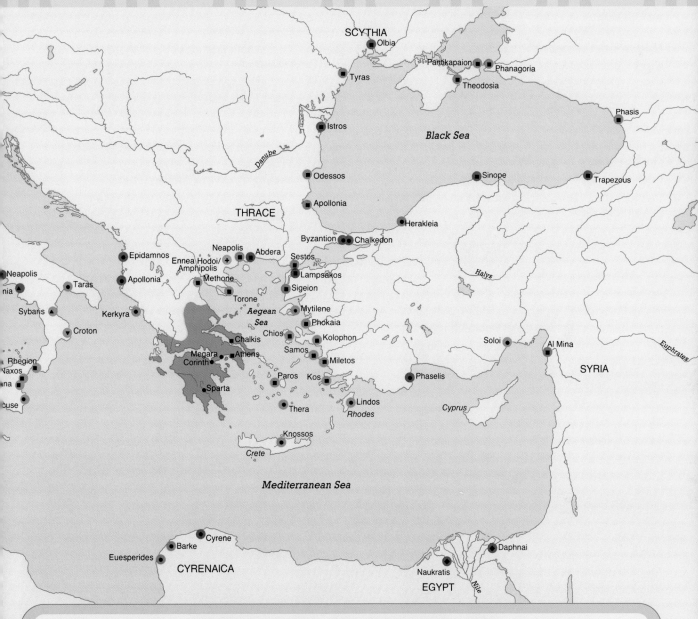

Greek colonization, 10th–5th centuries BCE

c.1050–950 Colonization of western Asia Minor from mainland Greece.

Late 8th century Early Greek colonies in the west. Naxos, Syracuse, Catana in Sicily, and Sybaris, Taras, and Croton in southern Italy. Colonies multiply, dominating the coasts of the area.

Mid-7th century Megara founds Byzantion, well placed to control the entrance to the Black Sea.

c.630 Thera founds Cyrene in North Africa.

Mid-7th–early 6th century Miletos rings the Black Sea with its colonies.

Late 7th century Naukratis founded: a Greek trading post in Egypt.

c.600 Phokaia (city-state in western Asia Minor) founds Massalia in southern Gaul.

c.510 Sybaris destroyed by Croton.

Mid-460s Disastrous attempt of Athenians and others to found large colony at Ennea Hodoi near coast of northern Aegean.

440s–430s Athenians establish colonies north of the Aegean.

MAGNA GRAECIA AND THE TYRANTS

Magna Graecia was the name given to the Greek colonies of Sicily and southern Italy. The Greek colonists of Magna Graecia became so rich and powerful that the Greeks back home in Greece envied them.

The Legendary City of Sybaris

Sybaris was a Greek colony on the east coast of southern Italy. It was such a wealthy city that its wealth prompted all kinds of stories and exaggerations. Other Greeks claimed that the citizens of Sybaris (known as "Sybarites," from which the English word *sybaritic* comes) lived lives of such untold luxury that they slept on beds of rose petals. They also claimed that noisy crafts such as carpentry were banned during the day because the Sybarites were accustomed to taking a nap to sleep off the effects of their late-night drinking parties.

Sybaris was just one of the wealthy western Greek cities. Unfortunately, it was destroyed in the 6th century during a war, but the ruins of its colony Poseidonia (Paestum), on the western coast of southern Italy, still remain today. It is notable for its columned temples.

Gelon, Tyrant of Sicily

Tyrants (*tyrannos*) were strong men or autocrats who ruled their cities with a tight grip. They usually favored the hoplites (or foot soldiers) over the aristocrats. One exception to this was the tyrant Gelon, who ruled the city of Gela on the south coast of the island of Sicily.

Gelon had his eye on Syracuse on the east coast of the island because of its large natural harbor. He took the city and made it his capital,

The Temple of Hera was built by Greek colonists at Paestum in southern Italy in about 550 BCE.

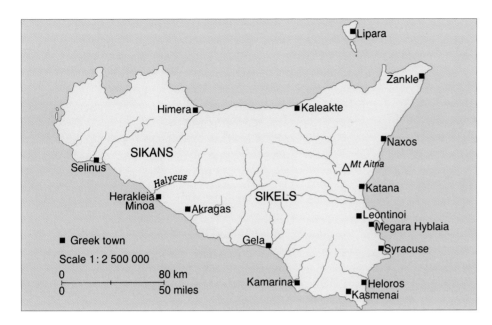

Colonies in Sicily. The Greek cities were mainly in the east of the island—the side that colonists sailing from the homeland would reach first. Syracuse sucked in people and power from neighboring cities, and even conquered a great Athenian force in 413 BCE.

forcing many inhabitants of Gela and other cities to move to Syracuse. Carthage sent a huge force to invade Sicily, but Gelon's army destroyed the Carthaginians in 480 BCE at Himera on the northern coast. The prisoners that Gelon took were made to build the great temples of Akragas, the ruins of which can still be seen today.

Tyrants in other colonies behaved differently. Kypselos, who was the first tyrant of Corinth, put down the aristocrats in his city, while Pittakos, the tyrant of Mytilene, disliked the drunken behavior of the aristocrats. Anyone who committed a crime when drunk was given a double punishment, one for the crime and one for being drunk. Peisistratos, the tyrant of Athens, expelled many of the aristocrats, but was known to be a fair and just ruler.

The tyrannies in the Greek homeland and Magna Graecia, from the seventh to the fifth centuries BCE. The age of the tyrants saw much prosperity, with fine buildings and, in Athens and Corinth, magnificent pottery. With many enemies among their own citizens, tyrants of different cities cooperated with each other rather than making war on one another.

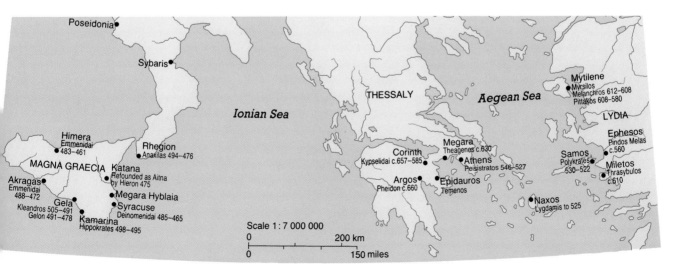

THE SPARTANS

The Spartans were a warlike people who lived in the southern Peloponnese. They took control of the fertile Lakonia region early on and then went on to take Messenia, in the west, during the middle of the seventh century BCE. This gave the Spartans control of a large region of the southern Peloponnese. Eventually, the Spartans would control most of Greece.

Slaves in Sparta—the Helots

"Helots" was the name given to the defeated people of Lakonia and Messenia. The Spartans were known for their fierceness and they treated the helots like slaves. The helots were forced to work in the fields growing crops, while the women had to make clothes.

The helots hated their new masters and the Spartans knew this. There were also a lot more helots than Spartans. To stop the helots from fighting back and to set an example, the Spartans gave up their drinking and their decadent lifestyle. Instead, they lived like soldiers, making sure they were always ready to fight.

The Spartan Army

At the heart of Sparta was the discipline and hard work that made their army the most feared fighting force in Greece. The Spartans spent their days improving their techniques for war. They employed various different strategies to instil fear and respect in their enemies.

They invented a series of maneuvers to outwit their enemies on the battlefield. They trained very hard and allowed others to watch their training sessions. This was a clever tactical move that succeeded in scaring their potential

Spartan hoplites gaze into enemy territory. Before invading, their commander will check whether or not the gods approve of the venture. He will sacrifice a goat and then examine its guts for "good" or "bad" signs.

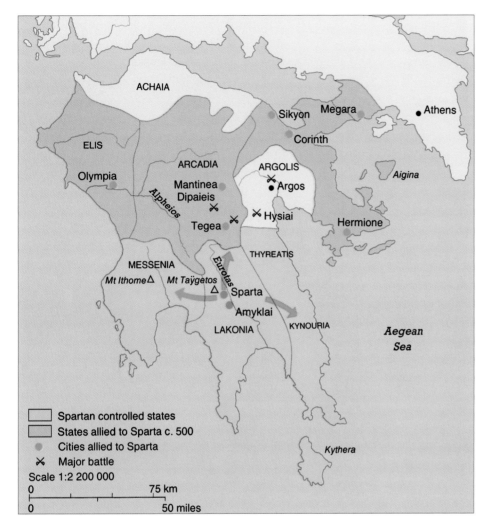

The Peloponnese with Lakonia, Sparta's homeland. In the mid-sixth century BCE, Sparta dominated most of the Peloponnese. By the end of the century the Spartans were ready to strike out into central Greece—against Athens.

Map labels:
ACHAIA
Sikyon, Megara, Athens
ELIS, Corinth
ARCADIA, ARGOLIS, Aigina
Olympia, Mantinea, Argos
Alpheios, Dipaieis
Tegea, Hysiai, Hermione
THYREATIS
MESSENIA, Eurotas
Mt Ithome, Mt Taÿgetos, Sparta
Amyklai
LAKONIA, KYNOURIA, Aegean Sea
Kythera

Legend:
☐ Spartan controlled states
☐ States allied to Sparta c. 500
● Cities allied to Sparta
✕ Major battle
Scale 1:2 200 000
0 ——— 75 km
0 ——— 50 miles

enemies. The Spartan soldiers also grew their hair long to make them look more scary. They rode on horseback into battle, while the helots were foot soldiers. The extra height gave the Spartans an advantage. They also learned how to move at night without using torches. The Spartans forbade the helots from going out at night, so they could not plot against them. The Spartans killed any helots found out at night.

Control over Neighboring States

The Spartans had to prevent the helots from joining forces with any potential enemy, especially those that might attack from the north. So, the Spartans used their army to establish pro-Spartan governments in the central and northern Peloponnese regions. They were supposed to protect the Spartans, but the tactic had mixed results. The government of Tegea promised to support the Spartans, while the powerful state of Argos remained an enemy.

In 494 BCE, Kleomenes, a Spartan king, tricked an army from Argos. He knew that the Argives (people from Argos) could hear when he called out orders to his army. He shouted out that it was time to eat. The Argives heard this and decided to eat, too. In fact, Kleomenes had secretly told his men to get ready to attack the Argives, which they did and easily won.

In 464 BCE, the helots started a revolt that lasted nine years. Finally, in 369 BCE, the helots of Messenia finally won their freedom.

SPARTAN LIFE

Life in Sparta was very hard. Our adjective "spartan" comes directly from the daily life of those ancient peoples and means "simple" and "frugal." To toughen up Spartan boys, they had to walk barefoot and wear few clothes, even in cold weather. They were kept hungry and were encouraged to steal food. However, if they were caught, they were beaten and told to steal more carefully next time.

These techniques were meant to equip the Spartan soldier with the strength and ability to fight the helots and to stop the helots from escaping. Hunting helots might mean surviving in cold temperatures and living off stolen food for several days. When they finally caught a band of helots, there would be fierce fighting.

Spartan boys were taught to respect their elders and follow orders. The army functioned by forcing soldiers to immediately obey orders, especially on the battlefield.

Fear of Family Life

Spartan rulers believed that a family unit could threaten the stability of Spartan life. Boys who were training as soldiers slept together at night rather than returning to their families. Young

Spartan boys playing a rough game. Spartans were taught to look on the bright side of death. A brave death in battle was a source of pride to relatives. The bodies and graves of brave men were displayed to make young people feel at ease with the sight. If a king died far away in war, his body was brought home preserved in honey for burial in Sparta.

married couples could not be seen together during the day. Husband and wife were not meant to be close, so Spartan men ate together in army messes away from their families.

By keeping families apart, the Spartans felt that they could make people be loyal to the state rather than their family. Spartan boys were educated to be loyal to the community. The name for the Spartan citizens was *homoioi*, which means "the men who are similar."

Scorning Weakness

No other people lived like the Spartans. The citizens of Athens lived in a much more relaxed way. At religious festivals, people there drank wine and got drunk. The Spartans disapproved of drinking, as they believed it would weaken the security of their city. Humiliation featured heavily in Spartan life. The rulers thought that by humiliating its citizens they would behave better. A man who would not fight, for example, was called a "trembler" and forced to shave one side of his face and keep a beard on the other so that people could instantly tell.

Spartan women, in contrast, were freer than women in other Greek states. They were educated, could own property and managed the farms when the men were away at war.

The ruins of an ancient theater stand near the site of ancient Sparta, which lay at the head of a long river-plain in a position protected by spectacular barriers of mountains.

ATHENS AND DEMOCRACY

The history of Attica dates back to prehistoric times when the region was made up of many independent villages. According to legend, King Theseus united the villages into one state. Its capital was Athens and its citizens, most of whom lived in the country, were known as Athenians.

The Akropolis

The settlement of Athens grew up around a great rock that loomed over the surrounding area. The Akropolis ("high city") was the main focus of the unified state. Its superb location commanded far-reaching views of the land and sea, allowing the Athenians to see any enemies and potential attacks. A fortress was built on the Akropolis, which offered protection from the enemy. The steep sides of the rock were hard to climb and the Athenians could attack the enemy with boulders, stones, spears, and arrows.

Athens in the early historical period, sixth–fifth centuries BCE

Late 590s A bitter quarrel between rich and poor of Athens is solved. Spared a civil war, Athens has the strength to expand. Not long afterward, Athenians capture the island of Salamis from neighboring Megara (see map). Peisistratos commands the victorious forces.

c.546 At the third attempt, Peisistratos manages to make himself sole ruler ("tyrant") of Athens. Under the tyranny, fine buildings and beautiful painted pottery are made.

c.510 The tyranny ends in blood. Hippias, Peisistratos's son, who killed many citizens, is thrown out.

508–507 Beginnings of a new revolutionary style of government—*demokratia*, the rule of the people.

Late 480s A big new supply of silver is found in Athens' mines at Laureion. The Athenians decide to spend it on building a large fleet of warships. This is just in time, because ...

480–479 ... Persia invades Greece with an enormous fleet and army (see pages 34-35). Although defeated, the Persians destroy much of Athens.

479 onward Athenians return and hurriedly build a great defensive wall around their city, and fortify a new port. It will become the most famous in the Mediterranean—Peiraieus.

Socrates made himself unpopular by asking difficult questions, such as "What is true justice?" and "What does 'knowledge' mean?" People could not answer and were embarrassed. Condemned to death for "corrupting the young" and "introducing new gods," Socrates refused to escape and died by drinking poison in 399 BCE.

The Beginning of "People Power"

The philosopher Aristotle wrote that every Greek state contained a few rich people and a lot of poor people. Rich and poor often fought against each other, sometimes with civil war breaking out. Greeks called this conflict *stasis*, and many states were weakened by it. Both Athens and Sparta managed to avoid *stasis*, which perhaps explains how these states grew so powerful.

Rich Spartan landowners ruled with an iron hand. They scared the poor into obedience and

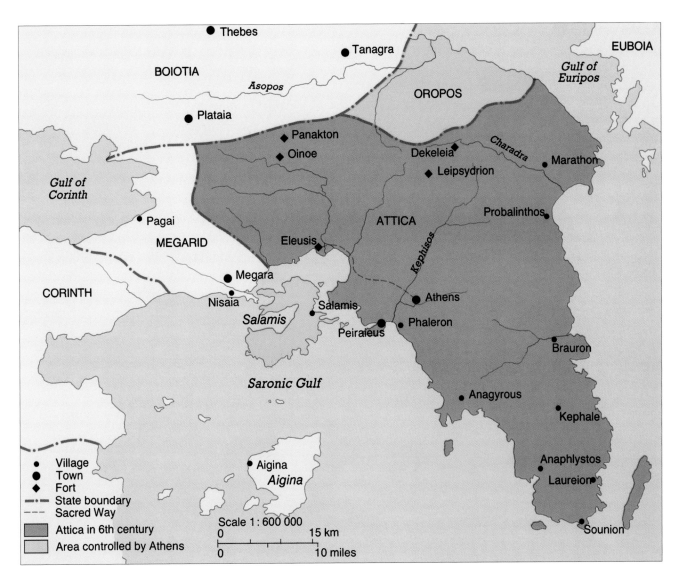

Map legend:
- Village
- Town
- Fort
- State boundary
- Sacred Way
- Attica in 6th century
- Area controlled by Athens

Scale 1 : 600 000

0   15 km

0   10 miles

Attica became wealthy from producing olive oil. Silver from mines at Laureion enriched Athens and made its coins. By conquering the great islands of Salamis (early sixth century B.C.E.) and Aigina (mid-fifth century), Athens made safe its profitable seaborne trade into Phaleron and Peiraieus.

treated them no better than the helots and slaves. In Athens, the poor were treated much better. They had more freedom and power. The poor controlled the main decision-making bodies—the assembly and the law courts. This system was largely invented in Athens and was called *demokratia*. *Demos* means "the ordinary people" and *kratos* means "power."

The rich tolerated this situation because they played an important role in influencing the poor to make decisions. The rich men, who had the best education and had learned the art of public speaking, would address a crowd of ordinary people to persuade them. Any topic of concern, from "Shall we go to war?" to "How shall we spend the city's money?" or "What taxes should we pay?" was debated at these gatherings and then decided upon by voting. Thousands of ordinary citizens in the assembly met on a hillside near the Akropolis where they would cast their vote. Every citizen, whether rich or poor, had one vote each.

Athens

As the defeated Persians left Athens in 479 BCE, they showed their anger by destroying much of the city. When the Athenians returned, having been away from Athens for a year, they set about rebuilding their city and within 50 years they had transformed Athens into the most splendid of all Mediterranean cities.

Rebuilding the City Wall
Before the Athenians started to rebuild their city, they built a huge circular wall to defend against future attacks. Working quickly, they were able to complete the wall before the Spartans brought an army to stop them.

Themistokles was one of Athens' cleverest politicians. He thought that the Athenians should move their capital from Athens to the nearby port of Peiraieus, where much of their food arrived by ship. He was worried an enemy might surround Athens and cut off the city.

However, Themistokles helped the Athenians to rebuild their city by tricking the Spartans into not attacking Athens until the wall was finished.

The "Long Walls" to Peiraieus
The people of Athens were extremely loyal, not just to their city, but to the large rock of the Akropolis. It was where festivals were held and where they worshipped the city's patron goddess Athena, whose shrine was located on the top.

To further enhance the security of the city, the Athenians built a wall to defend the port of Peiraieus and then, in the early 450s BCE, they built a walled corridor from Peiraieus to Athens. The long parallel walls of the corridor protected Athenians and goods as they traveled between the city and the port.

The Akropolis of ancient Athens seen today, with the Parthenon (top left) still partially intact. The temple was dedicated to Athena, the city's patron goddess.

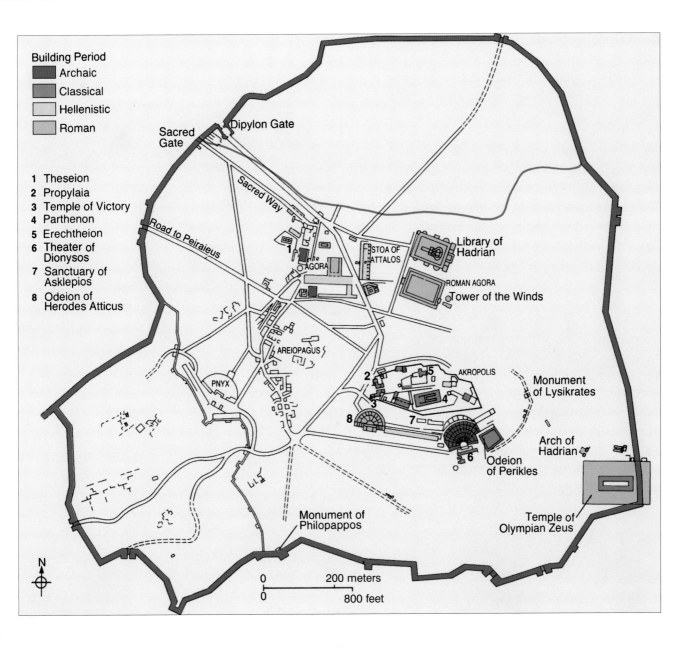

Building Period
- Archaic
- Classical
- Hellenistic
- Roman

1 Theseion
2 Propylaia
3 Temple of Victory
4 Parthenon
5 Erechtheion
6 Theater of Dionysos
7 Sanctuary of Asklepios
8 Odeion of Herodes Atticus

Sacred Gate
Dipylon Gate
Sacred Way
Road to Peiraieus
STOA OF ATTALOS
Library of Hadrian
AGORA
ROMAN AGORA
Tower of the Winds
AREIOPAGUS
PNYX
AKROPOLIS
Monument of Lysikrates
Odeion of Perikles
Arch of Hadrian
Monument of Philopappos
Temple of Olympian Zeus

0   200 meters
0   800 feet

N

The Akropolis: Symbol of Power

When the rebuilding of Athens got underway in the early 440s BCE, the Athenians decided to build a new temple out of marble on top of the Akropolis. The Parthenon was dedicated to the goddess Athena and much of it still stands today. It was finished in 432 BCE, and people came from afar to see its beautiful architecture, which suggested power and wealth. Seeing that the Athenians could spend so much money on this, other Greeks wondered about how much

The Akropolis and its surroundings at the heart of ancient Athens. The plan shows buildings from several periods. Close to the Akropolis are the Pnyx (where the assembly met), the theater of Dionysos, and the murder court, the Areiopagos.

money they had to spend on warfare. The splendid building bolstered the image of Athens to the outside world. The city became a popular visitor destination. It attracted leading thinkers, such as Aristotle, who came to study at the academy of the famous philosopher Plato.

The Akropolis

The Akropolis looms over Athens. The highest point in the city was chosen as the site for a temple to the goddess Athena. The Akropolis was also used for the many outdoor festivals that the ancient Athenians held. Families dressed up in their best clothes and climbed up the rock, where they enjoyed free meat. Animals were sacrificed on the Akropolis during festivals. Meat was a luxury because there was little good quality grazing land and so the chance to eat meat at the festivals was a very special treat.

Opposition to the New Building

Between 450 and 404 BCE, a number of buildings were constructed on the Akropolis. The largest and most spectacular was the Parthenon. The building of the Parthenon was not without controversy. Some politicians said that it was not the right structure for Athens, because it looked like "a deceitful woman." What they meant was that the bright white marble with its small sections of brightly colored paintwork looked a bit like the pale face of a woman with bright red rouge on her cheeks. In ancient Athens, pale skin was a sign of wealth. Rich women stayed indoors, meaning their skin stayed pale. Poorer women often painted their faces white and added rouge to their cheeks to appear richer!

Historians think the real reason politicians objected to the Parthenon was because they wanted to pay for it themselves to increase their popularity and political control. Instead, the costs of the Akropolis buildings were met by the public—another example of how *demokratia* (democracy) worked in ancient Greece.

The Statue of Athena

The interior of the Parthenon was not meant to house worshippers. People worshipped outside. Inside was a huge statue of the warrior goddess Athena. The armor was made of gold and the flesh was ivory. However, this statue was not the public's favorite. The most sacred statue was old and made from wood. It was so highly regarded that a new building was constructed to house it. The Erechtheion was named after the famous king of Athens, Erechtheus. Female figures, carved from stone, supported the roof. In the open was the statue of Athena Promachos ("the defender"). Its bright metal could be seen gleaming by sailors far off at sea.

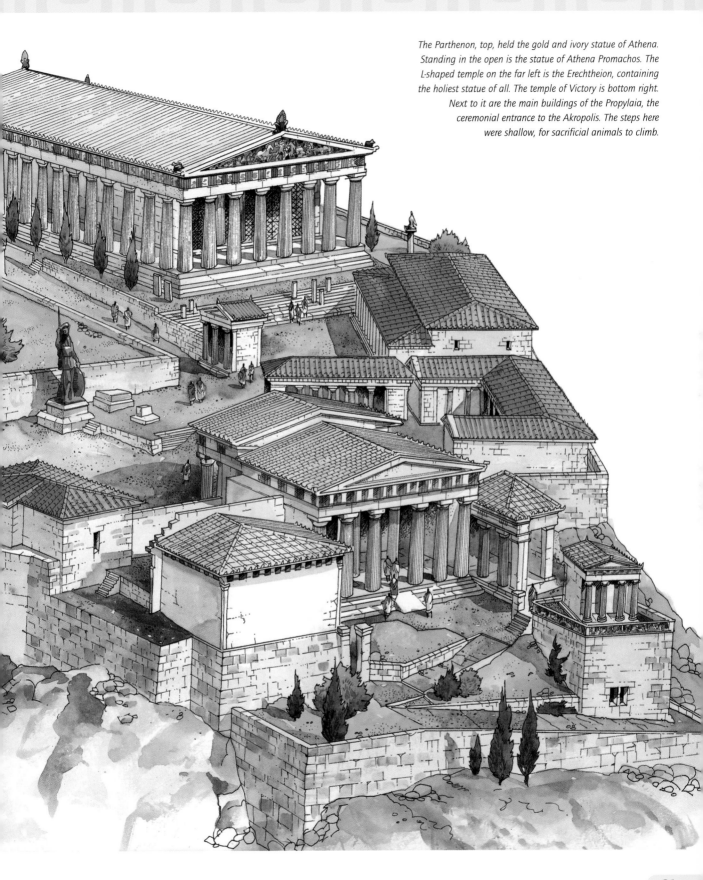

The Parthenon, top, held the gold and ivory statue of Athena. Standing in the open is the statue of Athena Promachos. The L-shaped temple on the far left is the Erechtheion, containing the holiest statue of all. The temple of Victory is bottom right. Next to it are the main buildings of the Propylaia, the ceremonial entrance to the Akropolis. The steps here were shallow, for sacrificial animals to climb.

EVERYDAY LIFE IN ATHENS

In its heyday in the fifth and fourth centuries BCE, Athens was the most cosmopolitan city in the Mediterranean, full of new ideas, news, and unusual objects to be bought and sold. At the port of Peiraieus, sailors arrived from all over the ancient world and many languages were heard in its streets.

Life in the Streets

Most Athenians were poor. The average person lived in a room made from mud bricks. An Athenian man would wake at dawn, covered in insect bites. He might then go to the market, as men did the shopping. On the way, he would pass slaves and women who carried pitchers of water. Only the richest houses had their own water supply. Everyone else had to carry water from a spring. There was no sewerage system in Athens, so the streets were full of sewage. Boys and men were far more visible on the streets than women and girls. When they were old enough, boys began work, although the sons of richer families went to school. Girls stayed at home and did not go to school.

Behavior of Citizens

Market traders were looked down upon and were protected by law from being insulted. However, freedom of speech was prized and poor men and even slaves were known to have stood their ground against richer men. One rich Athenian complained that even the horses and donkeys seemed to have self-confidence!

At the market, people met to talk. One topic of conversation was the price of food. Others who might stroll past included wealthy men, who talked about politics and religion. Many such men, such as the political theorists and philosophers Thucydides, Kritias, and Plato, did not like ordinary Athenians. They thought these citizens had too much power and were too uneducated to have a say in the running of the state. The poor resented their attitude and sometimes would punish a rich man for being anti-democratic.

An Athenian street. Lacking even simple machinery, Greeks carried burdens on their own backs. In ancient Athens, rich and poor mingled easily. In the streets of other cities, rich men swept the poor aside. Women escorted each other, ignoring the stares of men.

WAR AGAINST PERSIA

Persia was a vast empire that lay to the east of the Greek world. Persia extended from the shores of the Aegean Sea as far east as India, and from Russia to Egypt. The Persian Empire was far richer and had far more people than the Greek world.

For years, many of the Greeks who lived in Asia Minor belonged to the Persian Empire. Then, in the 490s BCE, some of them rebelled against their rulers. Ionians, who were led by the city of Miletos, rose up against the mighty Persian Empire. They were helped in their struggle by a force of Athenians who sailed across the Aegean Sea. The rebels managed to destroy the city of Sardis, the home of the local

Persian governor, before their rebellion was put down. In order to punish the Ionians for the insurrection, the Persians destroyed Miletos, mutilated its boys and abducted the most beautiful girls, who were forced to serve the Persian king, Darius.

The Battle of Marathon

King Darius wanted revenge on Athens for helping in the attack on Sardis. In 490 BCE, his Persian force sailed across the Aegean Sea and landed on the plain of Marathon, close to Athens. In the ensuing battle, the heavily armed Greek army easily defeated the lightly-armed Persians, who quickly fled back to their ships. A runner—a Greek soldier named Pheidippides— was sent from Marathon to Athens to tell the people of the city about the famous victory. He ran a distance of slightly less than 30 miles (48 km), the first "marathon" run in history.

- ⇢ Route of Persian fleet under Mardonios, 492
- → Route of Persian army under Darius, 492
- ⇢ Route of Persian fleet under Datis, 490
- ⇢ Route of Persian fleet under Xerxes, 480
- ⇢ Route of Persian army under Xerxes, 480

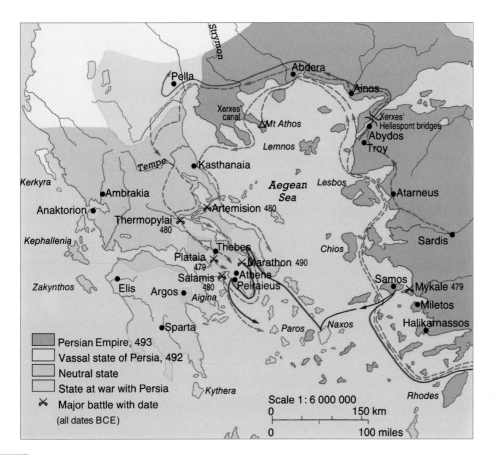

Persian expeditions. The invaders of 490 BCE sailed to Marathon. In 480 BCE, Xerxes' far larger force (land army and fleet) progressed along the coasts of Asia Minor and mainland Greece. To cross the Hellespont they made a bridge of boats.

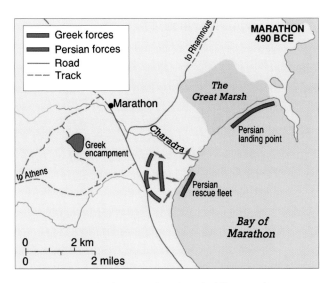

At Marathon, the Athenians came down from the hills to attack the Persians who had invaded from the sea.

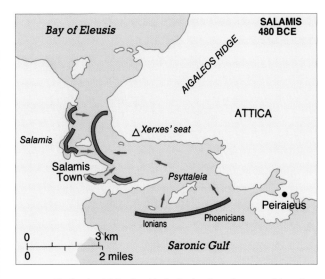

The battle of Salamis, with the Persian fleet about to sail into the narrows where the Greeks are waiting.

The Great Invasion of 480 BCE

Following two humiliations, the Persians were now determined to inflict a decisive defeat on the Greeks. Darius's son, King Xerxes, decided to invade Greece in order to finally settle matters. The Greeks tried to spy on Xerxes' troops, but the spies were caught and later sent back home to Greece to tell their leaders that the Persian army that was being assembled was so big and powerful as to be unimaginable. Herodotos, the Greek historian, estimated that the Persian army had more than five million men. In contrast, the Greek forces of Athens and Sparta had fewer than 50,000 soldiers.

The Greeks, led by the Spartans, realized that if the Persians surrounded them and cut off their supply lines then they would probably be defeated. They decided to fight their enemy in narrow places where the Persians would be blocked.

Firstly, they positioned their sea fleet in the channel of Artemision and placed their army in the narrow pass at Thermopylai in order to prevent the Persians from landing troops and surrounding the Greeks. However, in the hope of being rewarded, a treacherous Greek then betrayed his fellow men by helping the Persians by showing them a mountain track. This enabled the Persian to trap 300 Spartan soldiers under the command of their leader, Leonidas. The 300 Spartan warriors all died fighting against overwhelming odds, but, before they finally fell, they inflicted heavy losses on the enemy Persian force.

Xerxes' remaining troops were then able to pour through the pass at Thermopylai and went on to capture the city of Athens. However, when they arrived, they found that the city was strangely empty. The Athenian warriors had left and were waiting with the Greek fleet in a nearby channel at Salamis. Xerxes was probably then told in a secret message that the Greeks were quarreling among themselves at Salamis and that he should attack them quickly while they were distracted.

Xerxes fell for the ruse—but it was a trap and his fleet was easily defeated. The Greek ships were heavier and crashed into the Persian ships. Persian sailors were easily killed in the water. The Greek victory at Salamis was a turning point. Xerxes and many of his troops returned, defeated, to Asia. The remaining Persian army was defeated at Plataia in 479 BCE. The Greeks had finally triumphed.

The Persians, defeated at Salamis and at Plataia, gave up and fled back to Asia. However, the Greeks were not sure they would not attack again. So, they decided to attack the Persians while they were weakened. The Spartans did not want to carry on fighting, but the Athenians did. They knew they had the best fleet and that it could successfully attack the coastlines of the Persian Empire. So, the eastern Greeks turned to the Athenians to lead them against the Persians.

From 477 BCE, the allies of Athens had to deposit money into a treasury on the island of Delos in the Aegean Sea to pay for any future wars against Persia. Athens soon took control of the money and used it to pay for buildings in Athens. The Delian League, as the eastern Greek allies were known, became absorbed into the Athenian Empire. Not only did the Athenians have new buildings, they also had spare money to fight against other enemies.

War Against Sparta

The Spartans knew that the Athenians had grown stronger than them and they were worried that, one day, Athens would attack them. Sparta kept a close eye on Athens, looking for a chance to attack when Athens showed any sign of weakness. From 465 BCE, for 60 years, Sparta and Athens fought each other, on and off. These battles are known as the Peloponnesian Wars.

In the early 450s BCE, while Athenian troops were far away in Egypt fighting the Persians, the Spartans struck, defeating the Athenians at Tanagra, but they were unable to take Athens. The Spartans attacked again in 431 BCE, at a time when Athens was weakened by the revolt of many of its allies. The Spartans burned the Athenians' crops, while all that the Athenians could do was to watch helplessly. Although they wanted to fight back, the Athenians' strength lay in their naval fleet and not in their army. Wisely, their commander Perikles stopped them from fighting back, much

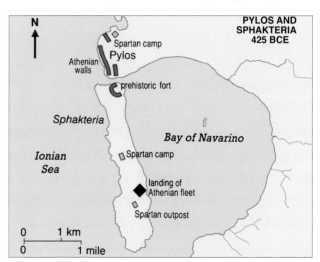

In 425 BCE, Athens put men ashore at Pylos. Sparta blundered by putting its own troops on the nearby island of Sphakteria, where the Athenians captured them.

A hoplite helmet. In battle, hoplites' heads had to remain exposed because they had to be able to look over the top of their shields. The helmets evolved to protect their faces and throats from downward spear jabs from their enemies.

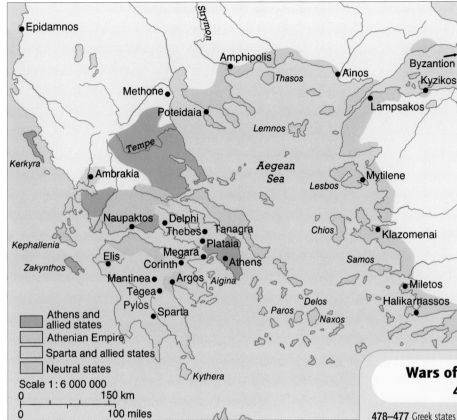

Epidamnos
Strymon
Amphipolis
Thasos
Ainos
Byzantion
Kyzikos
Methone
Lampsakos
Poteidaia
Lemnos
Tempe
Kerkyra
Ambrakia
Aegean
Sea
Mytilene
Lesbos
Naupaktos
Delphi
Thebes
Tanagra
Chios
Klazomenai
Kephallenia
Plataia
Megara
Elis
Corinth
Athens
Samos
Zakynthos
Mantinea
Argos
Aigina
Tegea
Pylos
Sparta
Miletos
Halikarnassos
Paros
Delos
Naxos
Kythera

Athens and allied states
Athenian Empire
Sparta and allied states
Neutral states
Scale 1 : 6 000 000
0   150 km
0   100 miles

The areas controlled by Athens and Sparta in the late fifth century BCE. Sparta's land army dominated its neighboring states. Athens' warships ruled the islands and the remoter coastal cities. The fleet guarded Athens' grain supply, which came over the Black Sea and past Byzantion into the Aegean.

to the irritation of the Spartans. Instead of engaging the Spartans in a big land battle, the Athenian navy took revenge by raiding the Peloponnese.

Sparta Allies with Persia

In 413 BCE, Athens suffered a disastrous loss when it lost half of its ships in a failed attempt to capture the Mediterranean island of Sicily. The Spartans sensed a chance for victory over Athens and made an alliance with Persia. Using Persian money, the Spartans built a fleet of their own. In 405 BCE, they successfully cut off Athens's grain supply that came by ship. The news was greeted in Peiraieus and Athens with wailing. After a year, Athens had been starved into surrender. The Spartans did not destroy Athens, but the city was now powerless. Its navy now had only 12 triremes (Athenian ships) and the Athenian Empire was finished.

Wars of the Athenian Empire, 478–404 B.C.E.

478–477 Greek states join Athens in the new Delian League, to fight Persia.

c.469 The League crushes the Persian navy at Eurymedon in southeast Asia Minor.

465 Sparta first plans to attack Athens.

c.460–455 Athens' attempt to capture Egypt defeated.

458 or 457 Sparta beats Athens at Tanagra, but gains little military advantage.

454–453 The League treasury is moved to Athens.

447 The treasury starts to be used to build the Parthenon.

431 Sparta starts the great Peloponnesian War.

425 Athens captures Spartans alive on Sphakteria.

413 Athens loses a huge fleet in Sicily.

405 The Spartan fleet cuts off Athens' supply of food.

404 Athenians, starving, surrender to Sparta.

SPARTAN EMPIRE

The Athenian surrender to the Spartans in 404 BCE marked a big change. The rich men in many of the Greek states were very happy, because they now had the opportunity to take control and to rule. They began by getting rid of the democracies that Athens had protected. Many democrats were simply sentenced to death and executed.

The Spartans also forced physical changes. They demolished the long walls that had linked Athens and Peiraieus and had protected Athens for 50 years from fear of a siege. As the walls came down, flute girls, who entertained the rich, played happy music.

The March of the 10,000
When the wars between the Athenians and Spartans finally ended, many Greek soldiers found themselves out of a job. In order to make a living, around 10,000 soldiers traveled to Mesopotamia (present-day Iraq) to fight as mercenaries for the Persian prince, Kyros. However, after Kyros was killed, the Greek soldiers did not have a master and found themselves abandoned far from home in the hostile Persian Empire.

The men marched northwest for around 600 miles (965 km) through bad weather and enemy territory, but remarkably few of them were killed. When they finally arrived at the coast, the men who were at the head of the marching column shouted in excitement, "The sea, the sea!" They had finally arrived at the eastern Black Sea, which is still a long way from mainland Greece, but that did not matter to them. Because they were a seafaring people, the soldiers had every confidence that they could now make it back to their homeland. After four months of seemingly endless marching, they were finally reaching the end of their ordeal.

Sparta's Defeat at Leuktra
The fact that the 10,000 Greek soldiers were able to march largely unscathed through parts of Persia suggested that the Persian Empire was weak. Although Sparta had taken control of the Athenian Empire, it attacked the Persians in Asia Minor with little success. The Spartans made more enemies than friends. Their way of ruling was not popular. They treated other Greeks with the same harshness and cruelty with which they had formerly treated the helots. Few Greeks would shed any tears when the Spartans finally met their match.

The Spartans attacked Thebes and Peiraieus, even during peacetime. In 382 they took control

The fortifications at Messene were built by the Thebans in the fourth-century BCE as defenses against the Spartans, who never managed to capture the city.

of Thebes. The Thebans resented Spartan rule, and as Spartan power diminished and Theban power increased, they were finally able to expel the Spartan garrison from the city in 372 BCE after a decade of occupation. Expecting a military response from Sparta, the Thebans gathered their army. It included the 300-strong Sacred Band, an elite fighting force put together from the best warriors in the army.

The Theban army met the Spartans near Leuktra in 371 BCE. When the two forces clashed, the Spartan king was killed and the Spartan line gave way. It was the Spartans' first known defeat in 400 years—and it brought the Spartan Empire to an end.

The march of the 10,000, 401 BCE. To fight his brother Artaxerxes, Prince Kyros employed a Greek army—the best soldiers—and Asian troops. They were led into Babylonia and won the battle of Cunaxa, although Kyros was killed. In spite of a truce, the Persians treacherously killed the Greek leaders, leaving the 10,000 to make their way home via the Greek cities of the Black Sea.

Three decades of Spartan rule, 404–371 BCE

404 Athens surrenders, and Sparta takes over the Athenian Empire. Democracy in many cities is replaced by oligarchy—the rule of the many by a wealthy few.

403 Democracy restored at Athens. Athens begins to regain some independence from Sparta.

401–400 The 10,000 march from the heart of the Persian Empire to the Black Sea.

396–394 Sparta campaigns against Persia in Asia Minor.

395–387 Athens and Sparta at war again.

387 Sparta abandons the Greek claim on Asia Minor and allows Persia to dictate peace terms for Greece.

382 Spartan troops seize Thebes.

378 Spartan forces try to seize Peiraieus.

371 Thebes's overwhelming numbers crush Sparta at Leuktra.

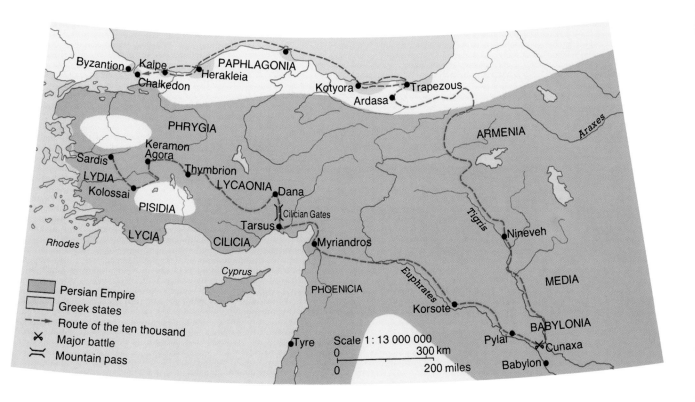

Byzantion • Kalpe • PAPHLAGONIA
Chalkedon • Herakleia
Kotyora • Trapezous
Ardasa
ARMENIA
Araxes
PHRYGIA
Keramon
Agora
Sardis • Thymbrion
LYDIA LYCAONIA • Dana
Kolossai
PISIDIA)(Cilician Gates
Tigris
Tarsus • Nineveh
Rhodes LYCIA CILICIA
• Myriandros
Cyprus
MEDIA
Euphrates
PHOENICIA
Korsote
BABYLONIA
• Tyre Scale 1 : 13 000 000
0   300 km   Pylai ✕ Cunaxa
0   200 miles   Babylon

▢ Persian Empire
▢ Greek states
- - -► Route of the ten thousand
✕ Major battle
)(Mountain pass

THE RISE OF MACEDON

Over time, the great empires that had once dominated the Greek world found their power had gone. The Peloponnesian War weakened Athens and when it lost its empire in 404 BCE it was fatally wounded. In the 350s BCE, Athens almost bankrupted itself trying to hold on to what remained of its empire. Similarly, Sparta lost its power after the loss of Messenia, despite unsuccessful attempts to get Messenia back.

With Athens and Sparta no longer a force, there was an opportunity for another power to emerge. Phokis, previously an unimportant state, and now the enemy of Thebes, stole the huge gold reserves of Delphi. The gold was melted down in order to make gold coins, which paid for mercenary soldiers for Phokis. These soldiers eventually defeated Thebes after a long war.

Situated in the northeast of the Greek mainland was the partly Greek kingdom of Macedon (Macedonia), ruled by King Philip. King Philip was very ambitious and probably took pleasure in seeing Thebes fall.

A modern statue of Philip of Macedon in the Greek city of Thessalonika.

Philip Conquers the Greek Mainland

Like the Phokians, Philip gained power because of his large supply of gold. The mines of Philippi produced enough gold from the 350s BCE onward to pay for a large mercenary army. The soldiers fought year round and were experienced campaigners, unlike the soldiers of most other Greek states. Those states could only afford to send out hoplites to fight during an emergency and their soldiers were only part-time.

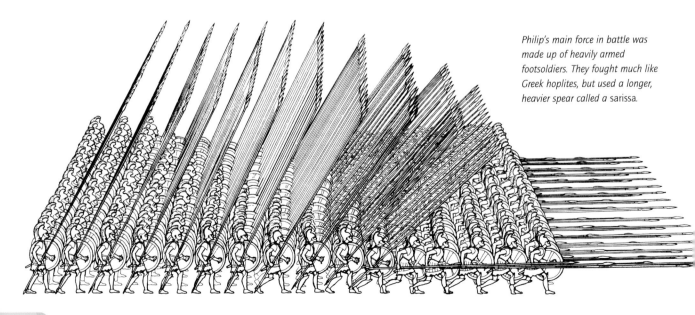

Philip's main force in battle was made up of heavily armed footsoldiers. They fought much like Greek hoplites, but used a longer, heavier spear called a sarissa.

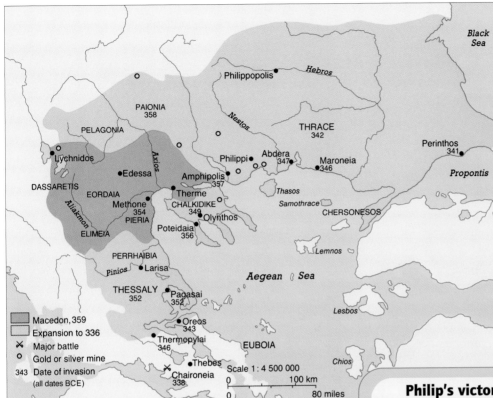

The expansion of Macedonia. The map shows how much the power of Macedon grew in the reign of King Philip (359-336 BCE). The area shown in brown was Philip's original kingdom. With his phalanx of infantrymen, he conquered territory all the way from the Black Sea to the Gulf of Corinth.

Philip's army fought in the east toward the Black Sea and in the south into Thessaly, greatly increasing the Macedonian state. They were helped by Philip's wealth. He used it to bribe politicians in other states to help him.

By 338 BCE, Philip was finally ready to attack the main Greek powers. He took his army south beyond Thessaly, through the pass at Thermopylai to Boiotia. At Chaironeia, Philip's soldiers fought the combined forces of Athens and Thebes—and Philip's forces won. With the victory, Philip's main enemy, Demosthenes of Athens, admitted defeat and Philip was now in charge of the Greek mainland.

Philip was a fair ruler, who wanted to keep Athens and Thebes on his side. He probably wanted the support of the Athens' fleet against the Persians. In 336 BCE, he returned to Macedonia, where he was murdered. His son, Alexander the Great, came to the throne. He would prove to be a much tougher king.

Philip's victories over Greece, 357–336 BCE

357 Philip captures the town of Amphipolis, giving him control of neighboring gold mines.

357–355 Athens loses a war to regain control of important East Aegean Greek states.

355–346 Helped by gold from the shrine of Delphi, Phokis wears down Thebes in war.

348 Philip captures and destroys Olynthos, a powerful Greek city close to Macedonia.

338 Philip's army of experienced pikemen conquers the hoplites of Thebes and Athens at Chaironeia. Philip is now the chief ruler in Greece.

336 Murder of Philip. Alexander comes to the throne.

Historians consider Philip's victory to mark the end of Greek independence, because Macedonian generals now ruled the region. Although the Greek states continued to fight between themselves, the Macedonians had bigger enemies in their sight.

Vergina

Archeologists working at a site in Vergina in Macedonia made an exciting discovery in 1977. They discovered underground tombs that had escaped looting. The tombs were obviously built for a rich and important person, probably even for royalty, because they were constructed of marble and contained the most magnificent treasure that anyone in ancient Greece was ever buried with. One tomb contained the remains of a skeleton and skull from a body that had been cremated. However, there were few clues as to whom the remains belonged to, because none of the graves contained any inscriptions.

Who was the Soldier in the Tomb?

Nevertheless, archeologists did have some information to work with. They knew that the Macedonian rulers were buried at a place named Aigai. They knew from historical accounts that the tomb could not be that of Alexander the Great, the most famous ruler of Macedon, because he actually spent little of his life in Macedon, living and dying on campaign. For centuries, his embalmed body was on display in the city he founded, Alexandria, in Egypt.

When scientists examined the skull found in Vergina they noticed a vital clue to identifying the individual. Above the right eye of the skull was evidence of a serious wound. Interestingly, an ancient Greek writer had written about King Philip of Macedon, Alexander's father: "His right eye was cut out when he was hit by an arrow while inspecting the siege engines and the protection sheds at the siege of Methone."

Historians know that the siege that the writer is referring to happened in 354 BCE. By all accounts, Philip was lucky to survive his wounds.

Further evidence found at Vergina suggested that it may well have been the resting place of the Macedonian king. The archeologists discovered an ivory model head in another royal tomb at the site that displayed an unusual groove over the right eye. This was likely a portrait of the king and suggests that the tomb was his.

Another Clue

The goods found in the tomb seem to confirm that its occupant had a military background. There was a large shield-cover and bronze leg guards, known as "greaves". Interestingly, the leg guards are of different lengths. One is about 1 inch (2.5 cm) shorter than the other, which fits with the known fact that Philip's legs were of different lengths. The leg guards may have been made specially for him and would have been buried with him in case he needed them in the next life.

Whether the skeleton and skull actually are those of Philip remains unclear—and may never be know for sure. Medical tests have not been conclusive and there is some suggestion that the remains might be those of a half-brother of Alexander. However, what is clear is that the tomb at Vergina represented an unusual and

Philip II on a second-century BCE medal. Philip gained power and reputation through wars against the Greek city-states. At the time of his death, Philip was in the early stages of a campaign against Persia.

The gold for this magnificent casket, which measures 13 x 16 inches (33 x 41 cm), probably came from Philip's private mine at Philippi. Inside were the king's cremated remains. Imagine the archeologists' excitement as they lifted the lid.

spectacular find, as it is very rare to discover unlooted tombs today. Vergina probably escaped looting due in part to the large mound of earth that covered the tomb.

Philip's Murder—Who Ordered It?

The manner of Philip's death remains a mystery. The king had been stabbed to death by one of his own bodyguards at his court in Macedonia, during the celebrations for the marriage of one of the king's daughters. The killer was himself quickly killed while he tried to escape, and so his reasons for murdering Philip were never discovered. Some historians suggest that Philip's wife and Alexander's mother, Olympias, ordered Philip's murder. Philip had had another son by a later wife, and they argue that Olympias was worried that this son might try to prevent Alexander from succeeding to the throne. Many other historians reject that theory as not reflecting any known facts about the murder.

Rumors that implicated Alexander the Great in his father's death began to circulate soon after Philip's murder. In fact, although Alexander undoubtedly benefited from Philip's death, there is no evidence to suggest he had anything to do with the murder.

ALEXANDER THE GREAT

On the death of Philip, his son Alexander became king of Macedonia. Few expected him to do well. He was only 20 years old, and very small. His enemies dismissed him as being "just a boy." Alexander had another problem. His father had left massive debts and Alexander had no money, but this did not stop him. He had huge ambitions and planned to defeat the Persian Empire. This idea was not that far fetched. The Greeks had beaten the Persians on several occasions. In 401–400 BCE, a Greek army of 10,000 men had marched unchallenged across the Persian Empire. However, until the reigns of Philip and Alexander there had been no army strong enough to conquer Persia. With Macedonia now controlling most of Greece, the chance to create a huge army became a reality.

Alexander in Egypt and Persia

Alexander's army of 24,000 men came from Greece and Macedonia. Alexander crossed the Hellespont into Asia Minor in 334 BCE. His

Alexander's men fight the war elephants of King Poros in northwest India. The animals were trained to trample their opponents to death, while shielding the soldiers of their own side. Fear of the war elephants was one reason Alexander's army eventually refused to go further into India. Alexander's successors swapped a huge part of their eastern territory for their own herd of trained fighting elephants.

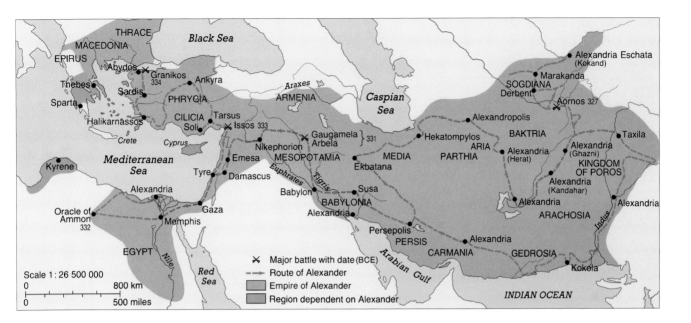

The conquests of Alexander. The army conquered an enormous area. By comparison, the Greek mainland is tiny. The soldiers marched so far partly out of respect for Alexander—they knew that he fought his enemies with utmost courage.

soldiers were heavily armed and well trained. Alexander won his first great battle against the Persians at the River Granikos. He then headed for Phoenicia, which lay at the heart of Persian naval power. He defeated the Persians there and then in Egypt. With these victories under his belt, Alexander moved further eastward to the heart of Persia's land power.

At Gaugamela, beyond the River Tigris, Alexander fought King Darius to take control of the Persian Empire. Darius had a far bigger army and chariots, but Alexander had trained his army well. Darius fled after fierce fighting and was killed by his own men. Alexander had conquered the Persian Empire and was now emperor. However, he did not stop there. His next target for conquest was India.

Alexander Advances into India
Alexander felt that if he took India, he would control the world. His troops defeated one Indian army, even dealing with their deadly

The reign of Alexander, 336–323 BCE

336 Alexander inherits the kingdom of Macedonia and overlordship of Greece.

335 Thebes revolts, but Alexander destroys it.

334 Alexander invades and conquers Asia Minor.

333 Victory at Issos—Alexander enters Phoenicia.

332 Conquest of Syria and Egypt.

331 Foundation of Alexandria in Egypt. Defeat of King Darius by Alexander at Gaugamela.

330–327 Alexander founds many cities in the eastern parts of the former Persian Empire.

326 Alexander enters India and conquers Punjab. His army refuses to go farther.

323 Alexander dies at Babylon. His empire is divided.

weapon—war elephants. However, the idea of crossing the vast Indian desert and fighting more elephants was too much for Alexander. His army would go no further. Nevertheless, Alexander's achievements were extraordinary.

Alexander was only 32 when he died of an illness. Despite his youth, he was always aware of the problems his new empire would face. The Greek-speakers had long looked down on the Persians, seeing them as uneducated barbarians, who followed their emperor without thinking. Now, as ruler, Alexander had to ensure he did not alienate the Persians or encorage them to revolt. One ploy he used was intermarriage. He married Roxane, an aristocrat from the East, and made many of his men marry eastern women, so that the future generation would be both Greek and eastern. However, this policy failed, as, after his death, many of his men divorced their wives.

The End of Alexander's Empire

Who would rule after Alexander's death? Typically, the intention was to produce a son and heir to prevent rivals fighting for control of the throne. Alexander's son by Roxane was too young to rule when his father died. Alexander's generals murdered both the son and his mother and split the empire among themselves.

Seleukos got the largest territory, which stretched from Syria and Palestine to India. It was Seleukos who gave up territory in India in exchange for 500 war elephants. Over the next two centuries, the Seleukid Empire, as it was known, grew smaller, but the elephant herd continued to terrify their opponents until the Romans crippled the animals in 163 BCE.

The kingdom that lasted longest was Egypt. Alexander's former general Ptolemy and his family ruled there until 31 BCE. The territory was rich, because the fertile banks of the Nile

The Hellenistic, or Greek, influence is obvious in the columns carved into the front of an elaborate tomb cut into the rock by Nabataean builders at Petra, in modern-day Jordan.

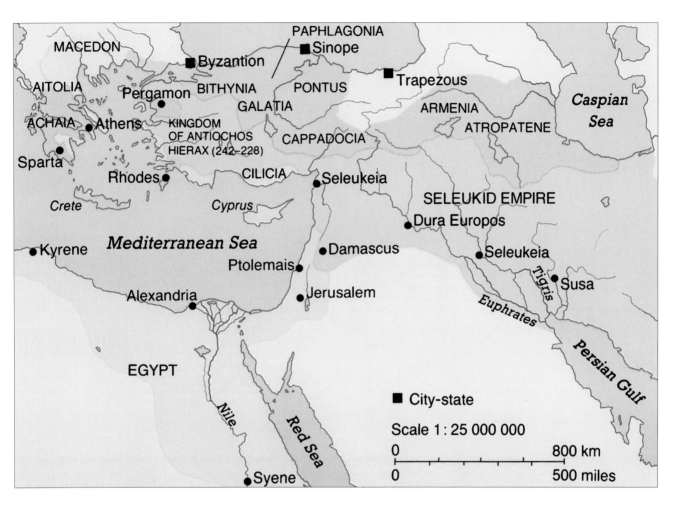

The map shows:

MACEDON
AITOLIA
ACHAIA
Athens
Sparta
Rhodes
Crete
Kyrene
PAPHLAGONIA
■ Sinope
■ Byzantion
Pergamon
BITHYNIA
PONTUS
GALATIA
KINGDOM OF ANTIOCHOS HIERAX (242–228)
CAPPADOCIA
CILICIA
Cyprus
■ Trapezous
ARMENIA
ATROPATENE
Caspian Sea
SELEUKID EMPIRE
Seleukeia
Dura Europos
Damascus
Ptolemais
Jerusalem
Alexandria
EGYPT
Mediterranean Sea
Seleukeia
Susa
Tigris
Euphrates
Persian Gulf
Nile
Red Sea
Syene

■ City-state

Scale 1 : 25 000 000

0 — 800 km
0 — 500 miles

The Hellenistic world in 240 BCE. The rulers of Macedonia have long ago lost control of the Asiatic lands conquered by Alexander, and also of much of Greece. Asia Minor has fragmented. But the Seleukids and Ptolemies still keep great empires.

produced a variety of crops. Under Ptolemic rule, Alexandria became the most important city in the whole Greek-speaking world. Queen Cleopatra was the last Ptolemy to rule Egypt.

The Greeks' Lasting Influence

The rich of the former Persian Empire adopted the Greek language. The poor spoke Aramaic, a non-Greek language. The most famous example was Jesus and his followers. However, when the New Testament was written, it was written in Greek. The Greek word for Greece was *Hellas*. Our word *Hellenistic* means "made Greek."

The biggest advances in the Hellenistic world were in science and technology. Among Hellenistic inventions were gears, cog-wheels, steam engines, and slot machines. Hellenistic scientists were very advanced. Eratosthenes was almost correct in his calculation of the circumference of the earth and Aristarchos understood that the earth went round the sun.

Even after the Roman Empire conquered most of the Hellenistic lands, Greek-speakers continued to exert influence, as Greek was adopted as the language of the educated in Rome. In 330 CE, the capital of the Roman Empire was relocated to the Greek city of Constantinople (previously Byzantion). One Greek legacy that did not survive was the idea of the city-state, in which citizens voted and served as soldiers as they did in Athens.

CULTURE AND SOCIETY

Greek society and culture influenced Western civilization for well over a thousand years. The philosophy of Aristotle and Plato, the democratic ideals of Athens, and the learning of scholars in a range of fields provided a classical basis for European culture throughout the Middle Ages; the Greek language was taught in schools until the 20th century, and Greek dramas are still regularly staged around the world.

The Temple of Athena at Paestum in southern Italy was built by Greek colonists around 500 BCE. Colonization and trade helped spread Greek culture and language widely around the Mediterranean and the Levant.

GODS OF OLYMPUS

Stories about the Greek gods and goddesses are still popular today. Tales about gods who fall in love with mortal women and goddesses who come to earth to fight humans' battles have been retold countless times over centuries. The stories have changed little since Greek times.

Explaining the Physical World

There was much about the world that the Greeks did not understand. They interpreted these mysteries as signs of the supernatural that were the responsibility of the gods. They wondered what lightning meant and why dark clouds brought rain. Phenomena they could not explain, they put down to the gods. The sky god Zeus was responsible for all that happened in the heavens, while the earth goddess, Demeter, was responsible for crops and everything that grew. If crops failed, the Greeks reasoned it was because Demeter was mourning the absence of her daughter, Persephone. The goddess Artemis was blamed if a woman died in childbirth.

Gods and Goddesses as Humans

When the Greeks tried to understand the powerful forces at work in the universe, they compared them with what they knew and that was the most powerful people of the day—the aristocratic rulers, who were almost always men. So, the chief god was male. The sky god Zeus was seen as the father Zeus. Since the early rulers lived on top of hills, from which they could watch their subjects and look out for enemies, the Greeks reasoned the gods must live high up. They believed that Zeus ruled from a palace on top of Mount Olympus and

Mount Olympus rises in the background behind a modern Greek village. In a remote, border region, the 9,500-foot (2,800 m) peak, often hidden among the clouds, was where the Greeks believed their gods lived.

was hidden by clouds. Aristocrats were often taller than others (largely because they had the best diets), and so the gods were thought to be tall. It was not uncommon for the Greeks to create statues of Zeus and Athena, his daughter, that were more than 40 feet (12 m) in height.

The Greeks believed that the gods and goddesses lived well on Mount Olympus, eating fine food and drinking wine. Just as aristocrats enjoyed love affairs with women of a lower social standing, so the gods were thought to do so. Zeus and his son Apollo were said to have had many mortal female lovers. Goddesses, however, had far less freedom, just as women in real life had little freedom. If a noblewoman fell in love with a man of a lower social standing, she would become an outcast in her society.

Nevertheless, ordinary Greeks did not want the gods to behave like mortal aristocrats. They wanted the gods to have their best interests at heart. The poet and farmer, Hesiod, imagined Zeus defending the poor against the aristocrats, while the philosopher Xenophanes did not like the notion that Zeus was like an aristocrat. Instead, he claimed Zeus was, "in no way like mortals, in body or in thought." Xenophanes

Artemis, sister of the god Apollo, was one of the oldest and most widely worshiped deities. She was the goddess of the forests and hills—where she was said to live—of hunting, and of childbirth. She was often depicted hunting with a bow and arrow.

thought that the gods were above the behavior of mere mortals. During the Classical Period, ordinary Greeks still believed in Zeus as the god of lightning, but they thought he used his lightning to protect the weak against the wicked.

Zeus was the ruler of heaven and the dispenser of ultimate justice. He sat on his throne on Mount Olympus, from where he fired his bolts of lightning. In most Greek myths, Zeus was a powerful and violent deity.

Delphi

Ancient Greeks, just like us, wanted to know what the future might hold. Today, we might perhaps turn to the astrology page in the newspaper to

read our horoscope, but the ancient Greeks did something different. They asked the gods. They believed that for a fee given to the priests, Zeus or Apollo would tell them the future.

The most famous oracle for telling the future was located in Delphi, high up in the mountains of central Greece. The other two famous oracles were even more remote from the main Greek cities. One was located at Dodone, far in the northwest of the mainland, and the other was in the North African desert. The more remote and isolated the oracles were, the more the ancient Greeks tended to believe that they were associated with the gods, who also lived far away on Mount Olympus. Delphi's setting was considered a likely place for the gods to visit as it was a remote natural setting.

How the Oracle Responded

The oracle spoke to ordinary Greeks in exchange for a small fee. At Dodone, the god spoke the future in the rustlings of an old oak tree, which people believed Zeus held to be sacred. Records kept at Dodone give us some idea about the sort of things that concerned the ordinary Greek person. Simple questions such as, "Should I marry?" "Shall I become a fisherman?" or "Did my servant steal from me?" could all be answered with either a "yes" or "no."

It was not just individual people who asked questions; a city might also pose a question, but it probably had to pay a larger fee. Often, the oracle was expected to give a long and detailed response. If it was later proved to be wrong, the oracle's reputation would be damaged and the oracle would lose business. So, in order to avoid

this, the oracle at Delphi became famous for giving answers that could be interpreted in different ways.

One good example of how this worked was when the Athenians consulted Delphi about the impending Persian invasion. The oracle advised the Athenians to leave their city, which proved to be good advice. However, just to protect itself, the oracle further added that only a "wooden wall" would remain. The Athenians puzzled about the meaning of this. Was the oracle talking about the wooden warships of Athens, or did the expression refer to a stockade made out of wood? By not specifying what it meant, the oracle protected its reputation. If the Athenians had trusted their naval fleet and it had been defeated, then the Delphians could claim that the "wooden wall" had not meant ships after all.

Apollo—the God at Delphi

Apollo was the god who prophesied at Delphi. A priestess, the Pythia, spoke his predictions. The Pythia was an older woman who had lived a pure life. She was chosen from among the poor people of the Delphi region by the priests. When asked a question, the Pythia would fall into a trance and then speak the words said to have been given to her by Apollo.

However, who was it that actually prepared the prophecies? The priestess was supposed to be uneducated, and much of the prophecy was cleverly written in very complicated verse. Any prophecy had to be both helpful and vague at the same time, which was a tricky combination to put together. The Delphians wanted to keep the answer a deep mystery and they always claimed that the words spoken by the Pythia belonged to the god Apollo alone and had come directly from him.

The ruins of a round temple, or tholos, stand at the edge of the remote site of Delphi. Like most of the other buildings on the site, the tholos has been damaged many times by earthquakes. When it was built in the fourth century BCE, it had 20 columns.

Olympia

The most famous shrine of the god Zeus was located at Olympia in the northwestern Peloponnese. Olympia was part of the state of Elis,

which had never been very powerful. Other states did not see Elis as a rival, and so were happy to send treasures to Olympia. It became a showcase for the Greek world and was used for religious and political purposes.

The Origin of the Olympic Games

However, it was the Olympic Games that brought Olympia real and lasting fame. Since the Greek world had no central government or capital city, war was a constant possibility, but once every four years, the Greek city-states agreed to a special truce so that they could travel to Olympia for the Games. These were originally a religious event, dedicated to Zeus.

We know about their competitive nature from a sculpture on the temple of Zeus (built in the 400s BCE), parts of which survive today. It shows a mythical chariot race, which some think was the origins of the Olympics. The myth told of King Oinomaos, who ruled a nearby town. He had a daughter, Hippodameia, whom he promised in marriage to any man who could beat him in a chariot race. Those who lost, the king killed. According to the myth, the king's horses possessed supernatural powers and so they could tell who might beat the king. After Hippodameia fell in love with Pelops, she feared he, too, might be killed. So, she arranged for her father's chariot to be sabotaged. The sculpture shows the king and Pelops just before the race, in which the king's axle broke. Pelops then killed King Oinomaos.

People traveled from across the Greek world to the Games and so Olympia became a show town. Successful athletes would put up statues of themselves and cities also used the Games to advertise their own triumphs in wars. So, for example, Athens reminded people of their victory at Marathon by putting on a show at Olympia, in which they "dedicated" the helmet of Miltiades, who had commanded their troops. In the same way, Philip of Macedon paid for a building at Olympia to house statues of his family and himself, after he had conquered most of Greece in the 330s BCE.

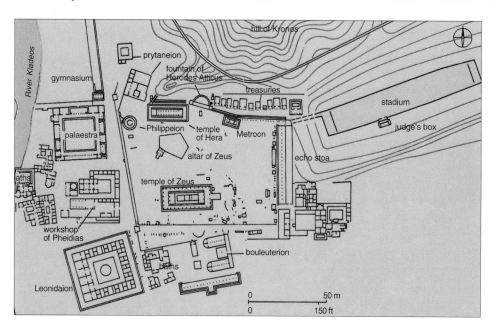

Plan of Olympia. The stadium (right) was the place for foot races. The palaestra (left) was the wrestling ground. Wrestling was a popular sport in ancient Greek and is still a part of the modern Olympic Games.

A few columns still stand of the Temple of Hera, wife of Zeus: the rest have been destroyed by earthquakes. The temple was the first at Olympia when it was built in about 600 BCE. Today, it is where the sun's rays are focused with a glass lens every four years to light the Olympic flame.

THE TRIREME

Warships lay at the heart of the Greek Empire. Many of the ancient Greeks lived on the islands of the Aegean Sea, just as they do today. The only way to get from one island to another and also to the mainland was by boat. Therefore, whoever controlled the sea, controlled the Greek world. The Athenians took control of the sea and were able to determine which goods and which troops went to which islands. To protect the merchant vessels that were bringing goods such as food to Peiraieus, the Athenians needed a fleet of powerful warships.

The Athenians relied on a warship called the trireme to patrol the sea and keep their trade routes open and protected. The trireme was a wooden galley, powered by up to 170 oarsmen, who sat in three tiers. The oarsmen were not slaves, but free men whose profession it was to work aboard the triremes. Each oarsman would have one oar, and by careful coordination of the oar strokes, the crew could generate a great deal of power and speed. Each Greek trireme was commanded by a captain called the "trierarch." He was a rich citizen of Athens, who would be helped in his duties by the deck and command crew, headed by the helmsman.

At its peak, Athens had about 300 triremes on the sea. The triremes did not carry weapons and they had room on board for no more than 30 armed marines, who, when the chance arose, might clamber onto enemy vessels at sea and fight hand-to-hand. However, the marines were not the main means of attacking an enemy ship. So, how did the triremes win battles and become so feared by Athens' enemies?

How the Triremes Fought a Battle

The triremes' main battle technique was to try to sink enemy ships. They did this by ramming the enemy ship's weakest part—its side. Built into the bow of each Greek trireme was a long wooden ram, which was covered in bronze to strengthen it. The ram was hidden from view, because it was under the waterline.

In a naval battle, the crew of the trireme had to ensure that the side of the trireme was not exposed to enemy attack. To prevent this, the trireme had to be able to move quickly, and the oarsmen, especially the helmsmen, became experts at maneuvering their ship. With their sides protected, the trireme would then aim to crash head-on into the enemy vessel. Rammed at high speed, the timbers of the enemy ship would shatter and it would then sink.

The Athenians' Tactical Mastery

In the mid-fifth century BCE, the Athenians' supremacy on the water was recognized by their enemies, who knew better than to attack Athenian triremes with their own triremes.

One incident clearly shows the Athenians' superior naval abilities. In 429 BCE, a small Athenian fleet was met by a much bigger naval force of enemy Peloponnesian warships in the Corinthian Gulf. To avoid being rammed, the Peloponnesian warships formed a circle with their bows facing outward, like the spokes on a wheel. Seeing this, the Athenian leader, Phormion, ordered his own his ships to circle round and round the enemy group. Growing nervous at this tactic, the Peloponnesian warships backed closer and closer together.

Then, as Phormion had fully expected, a sudden wind blew up. The enemy ships were now so closely packed together that the wind just added to their confusion. The oars and hulls of the Peloponnesian vessels began to become entwined, as the warships collided and became helpless. Phormion's triremes then attacked and the Greeks easily defeated the larger Peloponnesian force.

Triremes in battle. There was only a handful of armed men on deck. Most of the casualties happened when triremes, shattered by the rams of the enemy, spilled their men into the water. There they either drowned or speared "like tuna fish" by Athenian marines.

HOPLITES

The hoplites were the elite soldiers of their day and the most feared across the Greek world and eastern Mediterranean. They ruled supreme between the seventh and mid–fourth century BCE, because no foreign power knew how to match them. The name "hoplite" came from the Greek word *hopla*, meaning "arms." The hoplite carried these arms: a long spear for stabbing (but not throwing), a short sword, a helmet, and most importantly, a round, heavy shield that was made from metal and wood.

Typically, a hoplite had to buy his own equipment, but in Athens, if a hoplite's father had been killed in battle, the son would be recompensed by having his arms paid for out of the public purse. The wealthier the hoplite, the more equipment he would have. The wealthiest had the most equipment. Extras might include breastplates, leg-guards ("greaves"), and strips of metal to protect their thighs and groins. The poorest hoplites may have had to enter battle almost naked apart from their shields.

The Hoplites' Fighting Method

Heavy equipment weighed down the hoplite soldier, who could only move very slowly when fully dressed. Standing alone on the battlefield, a hoplite was an easy target for enemy archers, slingers, and cavalry that moved fast. If the hoplites were not organized, they were easy to attack. However, when they fought in the correct formation, they were virtually invincible.

As their strength and power in battle relied on them working together, the hoplites moved and fought in a close formation, known as a "phalanx." The hoplite soldiers stood shoulder to shoulder, so that their shields formed an unbroken line and their spears stood up close enough to each other that they looked a bit like the spines of a porcupine. On their own, each of

A hoplite was armed not only to kill others and to protect himself, but also to radiate confidence and frighten the enemy. The high crest of his helmet made him appear taller and stronger than he really was.

When opposing hoplites met face to face in battle, killing was done by jabbing spears downward at the face and throat. Shown here are various types of helmet, designed at different periods, but all meant to protect as much as possible of this vulnerable area of the body.

the soldiers could be attacked, but together they were unbeatable. There were several lines of hoplites in a phalanx. Even armed cavalry would think very carefully before attacking a phalanx of hoplites, because their spears could pierce both the horse and rider.

Importance of Shield and Helmet

What happened when opposing phalanxes of hoplites met in battle? How did they break through each other's phalanx? The answer is that they waited for any gap to appear in the enemy formation that they could penetrate. Once such a gap was exposed, the hoplites

rushed through the gap to attack their enemy in the undefended flanks and rear. The only way to prevent this from happening was to make sure that the line of shields remained unbroken at all times.

To do this, the hoplite held his shield in two places at the same time. His arm went through a loop behind the center of the shield, while his hand tightly gripped a handle that was fixed firmly behind the rim. However, the hoplite had to be able to see clearly over the top of his shield, which meant that he had to wear a helmet to protect his neck and head from being speared by enemy soldiers.

GREEK TRADE

The steep and barren mountains of much of mainland Greece and the lack of good quality soil across the region meant that it was often difficult to grow agricultural crops. Instead, most of the food and other supplies that were needed on the Greek mainland had to be brought in from elsewhere. From the earliest times, the Greeks traded with other groups, and most of that trade was by sea. Transporting goods by sea was often quicker than trying to cross the mountains that separated villages and towns.

Sea Trade with Foreign Lands

Of course, seafaring was not without its risks. Greek sailors relied on the stars to navigate by, but this was often dangerous. If it was a cloudy or stormy night, sailing became very dangerous. Similarly, only experienced sailors would know how far they had traveled and often even they would have no idea where potentially dangerous rocks might lay. Other threats to trade by sea included surprise attacks by pirates, who waited to ambush merchant ships. Pirates terrified the Greeks, as they were known to kidnap sailors

and sell them as slaves, as well as stealing the cargo of the ships they plundered. Pirates even threw sailors into the sea so that they did not live to tell the story.

As early as the Mycenaean period, Greek sailors sailed as far as Cyprus, Syria, and even northern Europe in order to collect copper and tin supplies. These materials were used to make the bronze that was needed for weapons and the armor worn by the Mycenaean soldiers. A wrecked ship from the Bronze Age has been discovered in the eastern Mediterranean. It was loaded with copper and was probably destined for a Mycenaean Greek town. The Mycenaeans traded with the Egyptians as well. The Greeks wanted Egyptian reed papyrus for writing.

A major import to Greece was food. When King Xerxes reached the Hellespont in 480 BCE as he invaded Greece, he watched the cargo ships, laden with grain, sailing through the

The main ports of Greek trade. Many products came from the Persian Empire, even though relations between Persia and Greece were often hostile. Grain carriers sailed from Athens right to the north of the Black Sea.

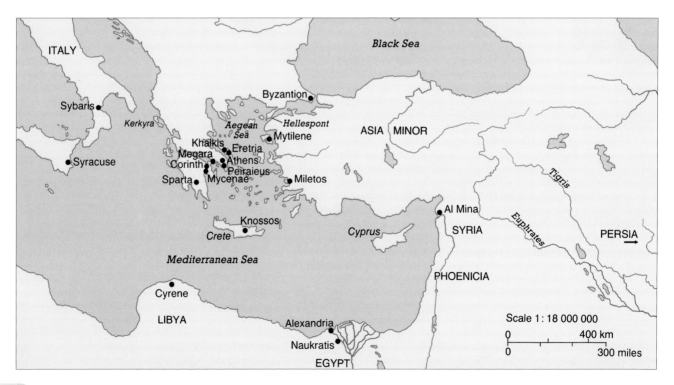

The Athenians also exported many of their own products, including olive oil, wine, and painted pottery, through their main port of Peiraieus, which grew into the most important marketplace in the whole of the Aegean Sea. Traders brought their goods to the port, which were then exported to many other Greek towns. Goods that they brought in included leather from North Africa, mackerel and salted fish from the Hellespont, salt and beef from Italy, sails and rope from Egypt, incense from Syria, ivory from Libya, dates and nuts from the central region of Asia Minor, and rugs and cushions from Carthage. Timber was another product Athens imported. It came from the lands to the north of the Aegean. Timber was vital for building the Athenian naval fleet.

The Greek Slave Trade

Slaves were another commodity that were transported by ship. The slaves could be Greek prisoners-of-wars, but more likely they were non-Greeks. The living and working conditions for slaves varied dramatically. One of the worst places to work was the silver mine of Athens. Accidents were common there and often the slaves were kept in leg-irons. Female slaves, and sometimes male slaves, were forced to entertain owners who could be drunk and mean.

The more fortunate slaves were those who worked as elementary teachers for the children of the wealthy, or those who worked as police in the assembly of Athens. A few slaves were rewarded for their service by being given their freedom, but for most, life was very hard and consisted of endless drudgery, such as fetching water or cleaning the homes of the rich.

There were as many as 100,000 slaves in Athens and the surrounding land of Attica. This number equaled the number of nonslaves in the region. Slaves usually belonged to richer people, but some farmers had slaves. Slavery was an accepted part of life in Greece and played a key role in the economy of most states.

In this fourth-century BCE carving from a funerary monument in Attica, a young girl stands before a portrait of the dead woman. Along with natural resources and trade goods, the Greeks also exported their artistic styles and craft skills, which spread widely.

channel. Athens, the largest city in the classical period, depended heavily on grain that was brought in from the regions along the Black Sea coasts. In order to protect its vital cargo ships, the Athenians built up a large military navy. They paid for the grain with silver from their mines.

GLOSSARY

akropolis "High city." A hill to which the citizens of a Greek town could retreat for defense. The most famous akropolis was at Athens.

archaic period The term now used for the time between the dark age and the classical period; roughly the 700s to the 480s BCE.

Attica The district surrounding and belonging to Athens. In its villages and towns lived most Athenian citizens.

Black Figure pottery This was made at Athens, especially in the sixth century BCE. The dark figures stood out against a reddish background.

centaur A creature of myth, with the head and torso of a man but the four legs and body of a horse.

citizenship To own land and take part in decision-making in a Greek state, it was necessary to be a citizen of the state. Citizenship was inherited. It was almost impossible for outsiders—Greek or foreign—to become citizens, though they might live there and be respected.

classical period The time between 480 BCE and the age of Alexander (330s–320s BCE).

Delian League The modern name given to an alliance of Greek states that was formed in 477 BCE to carry on war against the Persians. Its headquarters was on the mid-Aegean island of Delos. The power of Athens turned the Delian League into an Athenian Empire.

demokratia (democracy) A form of government in which the supreme power belonged to mass meetings of the demos (people). Many Greek states had it, especially in the fifth century BCE when the most famous democratic state, Athens, was at its zenith. The state most bitterly and actively opposed to demokratia was Sparta.

demos The citizen body, and especially the mass of poor citizens in a Greek state.

Hellenistic The name given to the Greek-speaking civilization that spread through many lands of the eastern Mediterranean and beyond following the conquests of Alexander the Great.

helots The mass of unfree citizens in Lakonia and Messenia, whose labor supported the Spartans. Fear of the helots turned the Spartans into a fiercely militaristic community.

homoioi ("the similars") The male citizens of Sparta who were deliberately educated alike so that they would have standardized personalities. Sparta had to be a harmonious community to resist its many enemies.

hoplites Infantrymen, armed with stabbing spears and round shields, who fought shoulder to shoulder, usually in a force that was several ranks deep.

Linear B The modern name for the script, composed of signs and pictures, in which Mycenaean Greeks kept records on tablets of clay.

millennium A period of 1,000 years. "The second millennium BCE" means the period from 2000 to 1000 BCE.

Minoan The name now given to the great civilization of Crete in the first half of the second millennium BCE. The word comes from the name of King Minos, a character of Greek legend who was remembered as having ruled in Crete before the Trojan War.

oligarchy Government of a Greek state by a few wealthy men. Oligarchs were of course strongly opposed to democracy.

ostracism An Athenian system of choosing between rival, highly influential politicians. Voters wrote the names of their least favored candidates on pieces of broken pot (ostraka), which were plentiful and valueless. The politician who received most votes against his name was ostracized, meaning sent into exile for 10 years.

Peloponnese The large landmass that forms the southern part of mainland Greece.

phalanx The battle formation of hoplites, shoulder to shoulder and sometimes many ranks deep.

polis The Greek word for a self-governing Greek city, town, or village. From this word come many modern words, such as "politics," "policy," and "police."

Red Figure pottery This showed figures in red on a dark background. Such vases were produced at Athens from the late sixth century BCE onward.

trireme A long Greek warship with about 170 oars, arranged in three banks. Its main weapon was an underwater ram at its bow.

tyranny Government by one man whose will was above the law.

FURTHER RESOURCES

PUBLICATIONS

Books for young people

Hewitt, S. *The Greeks* (Franklin Watts, 1998).

MacDonald, F. *Gods & Goddesses: In the Daily Life of the Ancient Greeks* (Hodder Wayland, 2002).

MacDonald, F. *Inside Ancient Athens* (Enchanted Lion Books, 2005).

McGee, M. *Ancient Greece: National Geographic Investigates* (National Geographic Society, 2007).

Pearson, A. *The Greeks* (Hodder Wayland, 1997).

Pearson, A. *Ancient Greece: Eyewitness Books* (Dorling Kindersley, 2007).

Picard, B. L. *The Odyssey* (Oxford University Press, 2000).

Powell, A., and P. Steele. *The Greek News* (Walker Books, 1996).

Renault, M. *The Bull from the Sea* (Vintage, 2001).

Schlomp, V. *The Ancient Greeks* (Benchmark Books, 1996).

Sheehan, S. *Illustrated Encyclopaedia of Ancient Greece* (Getty Trust, 2002).

Reference books for adults

Beard, M., and J. Hendersen. *Classics: A Very Short Introduction* (Oxford University Press, 1995).

Boardman, J., Griffin, J., and O. Murray (eds.). *Oxford History of the Classical World* (Oxford University Press, 1986).

Burckhardt, J., et al. *The Greeks and Greek Civilization* (Fontana, 1999).

Cartledge, P. *Alexander the Great* (Pan Books, 2005).

Cartledge, P. (ed.). *Cambridge Illustrated History of Ancient Greece* (Cambridge University Press, 1998).

Cartledge, P. *The Greeks* (Oxford University Press, 1993).

Cartledge, P. *The Spartans* (Channel Four Books, 2002).

Dillon, M. *The Ancient Greeks in Their Own Words* (Sutton Publishing, 2002).

Hansen, V. D. *The Wars of the Ancient Greeks* (Cassell, 2001).

Pomeroy, Sarah B., et al. *Ancient Greece: A Political, Social, and Cultural History* (Oxford University Press, 2007).

Powell, A. *Athens and Sparta* (Routledge, 1988).

WEB SITES

http://www.ancientgreece.com
World News Web site with lots of information about the ancient Greeks.

http://www.bbc.co.uk/history/ancient/greeks/
British Broadcasting Corporation Web site includes features and links relating to ancient Greece.

http://www.historylink101.com/ancient_greece.htm
History Link 101's ancient Greece page connects you to pages about art, daily life, maps, pictures, and biographies.

http://library.thinkquest.org/17709/indexe.html
Comprehensive site about ancient Greece.

http://www.museum.upenn.edu/greek_world/Index.html
University of Pennsylvania Museum of Archaeology and Anthropology Web site.

INDEX